The Journey of Faith

Sermons on Hebrews

Zane C. Hodges

Victor Street Bible Chapel
Dallas, TX

The Journey of Faith: Sermons on Hebrews
Copyright © 2011, 2016 by Luis C. Rodriguez
Published, with permission, by Grace Evangelical Society
Printed in the United States of America

All rights reserved. No portion of this book may be reproduced in any form without the express written permission of the publisher, except as provided by USA copyright laws.

All scripture quotations, unless otherwise indicated, are taken from the New King James Version®. Copyright © 1982 by Thomas Nelson, Inc. Used by permission. All rights reserved.

Hodges, Zane C., 1932-2008
ISBN-10 978-1-943399-11-6

Requests for information should be addressed to:
Victor Street Bible Chapel
4510 Victor Street
Dallas, TX 75246

This book is adapted from a series of sermons
that Zane C. Hodges gave to a church in
Southern California in July of 1983.

Contents

1. Never Give Up 7
2. Partners of the King 19
3. Suffering for the World to Come 31
4. Entering God's Rest 43
5. Saving the Saved 55
6. The Peril of Not Growing 69
7. The Secret of Success 83
8. The Journey of Faith 97
Scripture Index 111
Subject Index 115

CHAPTER 1

Never Give Up

Read: Hebrews 1:1-4, 13

Katarina was eighty-eight years old when she died just last March in a Philadelphia nursing home. Katarina's story is a very unusual story indeed. In 1921, the police found her wandering around the streets weeping and in fear. She spoke to them in sounds that were incoherent and they could not understand her. So, they took her to a mental hospital and Katarina was committed to this institution. For about the first six years of her stay there, she continued to speak in these unintelligible sounds. But in 1927, she stopped doing that altogether and she spent the remainder of her time simply wandering around or staring at the walls.

Eventually after forty-seven years in the institution, her commitment was reviewed and some language specialists succeeded in getting her to communicate with them. They made an amazing discovery. Those unintelligible sounds that she used to make were not unintelligible at all. They were an actual language. They were the Ukrainian language. The review committee discovered that Katarina had come to the United States at the age of fifteen from the Ukraine in Soviet Russia. She had met a young man and birthed a child. But then, both the child and the child's father had died, and apparently Katarina had suffered a nervous breakdown. It was in that condition that the police had found her.

Eventually, she was released and she spent the last thirteen years of her life in a nursing home under the guardianship of a daughter of one of the workers at the hospital. But, by this time, she was in her seventies. The very best years of her life were behind her and her experience in America had become a sad tragedy.

Katarina, I think, is an example of a person who gave up. She gave up, cursed by the loss of loved ones, living in a strange land, unable to communicate even with those who were trying to help her. She stopped talking altogether and spent about forty years of her life in silence. She gave up.

My friends, we are living in a world in which there are literally thousands of people who give up every year. Many of them end their lives by suicide, but others go through the motions of living, but without any real hope or any real joy. Let us face the fact that sometimes even Christians are tempted to give up. They are tempted to give up on their Christian faith. They are tempted to give up on the Bible. They are tempted to give up on God. If the time should ever come when you are tempted like that, then one of the most important books of the Bible for you to know and to understand is the book of Hebrews. For you see, the book of Hebrews was written to

Christians who were tempted to give up.

Now, we really do not know who wrote the book of Hebrews. Many have thought that the Apostle Paul wrote it and maybe he did. Or maybe it was written by Barnabas or by somebody else. But, whoever wrote the book of Hebrews, it is obvious that he was an inspired man of God. In a language that often rises to a tremendous level of power and effectiveness, the writer of Hebrews encourages his people to hold fast to the confession of their hope without wavering (Heb 10:23). He urges them not to give up their commitment to Jesus Christ and not to pass away their confidence in God. Naturally, because he has this in mind from the very moment that he set pen to paper, he is speaking words that are designed to encourage his readers.

From the very first paragraph of the book of Hebrews, I would like to confront you with some reasons why in the Christian life, we should never, never, never give up. The very first reason is this: God has spoken to us by His Son.

> God, who at various times and in various ways spoke in time past to the fathers by the prophets, has in these last days spoken to us by His Son (Heb 1:1-2a).

Does that excite you? Does that thrill you? Well, it should. What could be grander than to have God Himself communicate to us in the person of His beloved Son, Jesus Christ?

Some years ago while I was over at Dallas Theological Seminary, I was on my way to chapel one morning. It happened to be a day when the seminary boards were meeting and the members of the board were lined up along a narrow hallway that leads back to the entrance to the chapel platform. As I started down this hallway, I heard someone to my right say to me, "Hello, there". I turned to see who was talking to me and who do you suppose it was? It was Tom Landry, the head coach of the Dallas Cowboys.

Now, I know that I am in Los Angeles Rams' territory this morning. But, I want you to understand that in the city of Dallas, there are very few people with greater prestige than Tom Landry. I was a little flustered, and I managed to get out something like "Hi there" or "How are you" or "Good morning" or something like that, but that little incident made my day. Here was a man that millions of people had seen on TV with that fedora hat of his and that great stone face, pacing up and down the sidelines, sending in plays to America's team. I had not only seen him in person, but he had spoken to me.

Now, I guess I made a little bit more out of that incident than I should. If the man standing in that hallway had been Elijah, Elisha, Isaiah, Jeremiah, or Ezekiel, then that would have been greater still, because these men were great prophets of God. They were men through whom God spoke in times past to mankind.

However, even a privilege like that would have to take second place. It would have to take a distant second place to the amazing reality that God has communicated to me and to you in the person of Jesus Christ. You know, it is a wonder that when we pick up our Bibles that our hands do not tremble with awe and reverence, because in the pages of the NT are recorded the words and deeds, the life and death, and resurrection of Jesus Christ. Here in our hands, we hold God's supreme revelation. God has spoken to us by His Son.

Now I do not know whether at this church, you ever sing the little song about the wise man and the foolish man. It's called, "The Wise Man Built His House Upon the Rock." They probably sing it in Vacation Bible School. At Dallas in Victor Street Bible Chapel, however, we sing it often and not just the kids, the adults too. Believe it or not, the adults make the motions right along with the kids. Some of them had a little trouble getting over feeling self-conscious about it, but after they did that, they had fun. We enjoyed building the wise man's house upon the rock, and letting the rain come down, and the floods come up, and the house on the rock stands firm. But, it is even more fun to build the foolish man's house on the sand, to let the waves come down, and the floods come up until the house on the sand goes "Boom!" Everybody likes that.

That very clever little song is drawn directly from the teachings of Jesus Christ (Matt 7:24-27). He is teaching us that His Word is like a solid rock. If we build our life and experience upon the solid rock of His Word, then the storms of life will not overthrow our life and experience. But, if we build our lives somewhere else, we are building upon the sand. Life like that is destined for storm and destined for collapse. For the only firm place to build our experience is upon the revelation that God has made in His Son.

The writer of Hebrews believes deeply in the firmness of the Word of God. "Let us hold fast the confession of our hope without wavering, for He who promised is faithful" (Heb 10:23). One of the reasons in the Christian life, we must never give up, is because we can build our experience on the rock of God's Word.

The hymn writer got it right when he said "How firm a foundation, ye saints of the Lord, is laid for your faith in His excellent Word! What more can He say than to you He has said, To you who for refuge to Jesus have fled?"[1] In these last days God has spoken to us by His Son.

Now we live in a world that is very celebrity conscious and I need not tell you that in Southern California, do I? Whenever I come to Los Angeles, walk the streets of your city, or ride down Wilshire Boulevard, I keep my eyes open just in case I might see a famous face somewhere. I guess all tourists do that. Of course, advertisers know that one of the best ways to promote a product is to have a celebrity promote it. That is why Martha Ray talks to all of the denture wearers of America. That is why Lauren Bacall sings the praises of High Point decaffeinated coffee. That is why Robert Ludlum and Tom Landry and a host of others have told us never to leave home without our American Express card. Celebrities get it done.

In the person of Jesus Christ, we meet true celebrity. We meet true greatness. Here is someone who will someday possess and rule all things. Here is someone who made all things. Here is someone who perfectly reflects God. Not only that, He sustains all things. God,

> has in these last days spoken to us by His Son, whom He has appointed heir of all things, through whom also He made the worlds; who being the brightness of His glory in the express image of His person, and upholding all things

---

[1] John Rippon, John Keene, Kirkham, and John Keith, "How Firm a Foundation" (1787).

by the word of His power (Heb 1:2-3a).

Believe me, those are breathtaking words. Those are staggering concepts. Those are immense and awesome claims for the person of Jesus Christ. Look into the future. Look as far into the future as you can see. What do you behold? You see Jesus ruling all things. He is the Heir of all things. Look into the past. Look as far into the past as you can see and what do you behold? You see Jesus making everything. Look at the present. What do you see? You see the Son perfectly revealing God, and holding up the universe. Do you realize that you and I and everything in the creation are sustained every moment of every day by His mighty power? That, my friends, is true celebrity.

Last January, in Bel Air, an expensive mansion burned down. It happened to belong to Kareem Abdul-Jabbar. I guess I do not have to tell you that he is that seven-foot center for the Los Angeles Lakers, who is probably one of the greatest players ever to play basketball. His house burned down. It covered 7,000 square feet and was estimated to be valued at one and a half million dollars. The fire destroyed his extensive collection of expensive oriental rugs. It destroyed 3,000, I kid you not, 3,000 jazz records. It destroyed a whole bunch of trophies that he had accumulated over a long and illustrious basketball career. Kareem Abdul-Jabbar was in Boston with his team at the time it happened. When he got back, his agent was quoted as saying "He just got back. He's very upset. He lost everything." I do not blame him. I would be upset too. But here is a celebrity, my friends, who could not even protect his own house from fire. The fire wiped him out.

But listen. The Son of God will never be wiped out. He will never be wiped out. He made everything. He will someday rule over everything. Right here and now, He supports everything in the entire creation. Oh, how foolish it is for us when the pressures close in around us, when the troubles begin to mount, how foolish it is for us to despair and to give up hope.

The writer of Hebrews believed deeply that because of the greatness of Jesus Christ, we can come to the throne of grace and obtain mercy and find grace to help in time of need (Heb 4:16). One of the reasons why in the Christian life we must never give up, is because we can be helped by the Creator, the Possessor, the Sustainer of all things. The songwriter was right when he said, "He cannot fail for He is God. He cannot fail. He pledged His Word. He cannot fail. He'll see you through. He cannot fail. He'll answer you." Be sure of this. The One who upholds all things will have no trouble upholding you in your time of need.

But if it is inspiring that God has spoken to us by His Son, if it is thrilling that He who sustains all things, sustains us, here is something that ought to thrill us right down to our shoelaces. If you are not wearing shoelaces this morning, it ought to send chills right down to the tips of your toes. Are you ready for it? Here it is. Jesus sat down (Heb 1:3b).

I submit to you this morning that it is not only one of the central truths of the book of Hebrews. It is one of the most stupendous realities in the entire universe. For,

> when He had by Himself purged our sins, sat down at the right hand of the Majesty on high, having become so much better than the angels,

as He has by inheritance obtained a more excellent name than they (Heb 1:3b).

When Jesus Christ came into this world the first time, He came to deal with the problem of our sins. By His sacrifice on the cross, He purged our sins. He made it possible for us, by one simple act of faith, to receive eternal salvation, to receive eternal life, to have forgiveness of sins, and to possess the assurance that we will be with God forever.

Let me just pause to say that if there is anyone in this audience who has never trusted Jesus Christ in that way, your sins have been paid for. He invites you to receive Him as your own personal Savior, by a simple act of trust. Because He,

> became obedient to the point of death, even the death of the cross. Therefore God also has highly exalted Him and given Him the name which is above every name, that at the name of Jesus every knee should bow…and that every tongue should confess that Jesus Christ is Lord, to the glory of God, the Father (Phil 2:8b-11).

You see when the day came for Him to sit down at the right hand of God, God said to Him. "Sit at My right hand, till I make Your enemies Your footstool" (Heb 1:13). I want you to understand, that when Jesus sat down at the right hand of God, it was not only a sign that He had taken care of our sins. But it was God's guarantee, that ultimate, final victory would belong to Him. Sit until I make Your enemies a footstool of Your feet.

Not far from Chambersburg, Pennsylvania where I did most of my growing up, there is a place called Shippensburg and there is a state teacher's college at Shippensburg. One fall, they hired Jon Byron to teach computer science. What they did not realize was that on days that he was not teaching at Shippensburg, he was over at Millersville teaching economics as Peter H. Pierce. One day in March, as he was on his way to a class at Millersville, the police arrested him. Using a search warrant, they went through his apartment and they found sixteen boxes filled with bank records and identification papers and credit cards. They discovered that this man was known by at least thirteen different names in places like Britain, Canada, Australia, and the United States. There were letters in his belongings recommending the academic qualifications of Peter Francis Wendley, David Taylor, Keith Frederick Bowden, Kenneth John Holden, and George Spencer Vickers. It was not until later that the police found out his real name was Paul Arthur Crafton, and he taught for twenty-seven years at the George Washington University. Because they were puzzled about his real name, they registered him and booked him as John Doe.

What is in a name? Well, in this case, there is not a lot, not a very great deal. But even though the names that men use are often false and deceptive; even though they often hold out promise that they can never fulfill, the name of God's Son is full of divine reality. It is full of divine truth. Even though the angels are great majestic beings, and they are names to be highly honored. The name of "Son" is far above their names. For now, the name of "Son" carries with it God's promise of victory and of dominion over the entire creation. One of the reasons why in the Christian life we must never give up, is because, through Jesus Christ, we can be victorious, too.

Never Give Up 17

Martin Luther, coming through the fires of the Reformation with all of its struggles and danger, captured this principal perfectly.

> Did we, in our own strength confide, our striving would be losing.
> Were not the right Man on our side, the Man of God's own choosing.
> Doth ask Who that may be? Christ Jesus, it is He,
> Lord Sabaoth, His Name, from age to age, the same.
> And He must win the battle.[2]

To which of the angels, did He ever say, "Sit at My right hand till I make Your enemies Your footstool"? (Heb 1:13). He never said it to the angels. But, He said it to His Son.

Cora Lefler is a seventy-four year old widow who lives in and around Charlotte, North Carolina. She has seen her share of troubles. She has been beaten and left for dead. She has been robbed so many times, that about the only valuable possession that she has is her monthly social-security check. Her house has been condemned, and she carries her belongings around in a white pillowcase. Efforts to help her by friends and relatives and government agencies have been rebuffed because Cora Lefler is a very independent person. "I can take care of myself," she says. She spends her days cleaning up at the Belvedere Laundry sweeping out and carrying out the trash. At night, mind you, if she has fifty cents, she hops on a bus and she goes to Mecklenburg County Jail. If she

---
[2] Martin Luther, "A Mighty Fortress Is Our God" (c. 1529).

does not have money for a bus ride, she walks.

For the last four years, she has been sleeping every night at the Mecklenburg County Jail. Her bed is a wooden bench in the jail lobby. Psychiatrists say she is eccentric, but she is not dangerous, and as long as she is not dangerous, we have to let her do what she wants to do. The headline that reported this interesting item, read like this "Woman Seeks Refuge at Jail" and the sub-headline said, "Driven by a pact, seventy-four year old widow seeks unusual haven". Now that is a remarkable story about a very independent woman who knows where to go for refuge.[3]

I am not recommending Cora Lefler's lifestyle to anyone this morning, as I'm sure you will understand. But, you know it did occur to me, that in some way, intelligent and dedicated Christians are a little bit like her. We may be regarded by the world as eccentric, but we know where to find protection. We know where to find help. We know where to find refuge, because we know that God has spoken to us by His Son. We know that the One, Who supports the universe, supports us. We know that the final victory belongs to Him. Because we know all these things, we also know that in the Christian life, we need never, never, never to give up.

---

[3] Reported by the *Free Lance-Star*, Fredericksburg, VA, February 9, 1983.

CHAPTER 2

Partners of the King

READ: HEBREWS 1:6-9; 3:1, 14; 12:28

One Friday in October, police officer Robert Parrish of Trenton, New Jersey responded to a silent alarm at the Key & Inn Tavern. Going along with him on this call was Mack, his off-duty companion and his on-duty partner. Mack, however, was only two years old, which is not too surprising, considering that Mack was a member of the Trenton Canine Unit. He was a black and tan German shepherd. When they arrived at the tavern, Robert Parrish took Mack inside for inspection of the premises. Mack led to a doorway cellar, which was closed but not locked. They went down together into the cellar. But as Parrish reached for the light switch to turn the lights on, suddenly a knife wielding seventeen year old teenager leaped out from behind a partition.

Instantly, Mack was on his arm, but was slashed for his trouble. Mack hardly knew he had been hit and he moved in again for a second attack. By this time, Parrish had been able to draw his gun and he disarmed the young teenager. But, Mack was seriously hurt. He was rushed to an animal hospital. There on an operating table, Mack died while his partner embraced him with his blue uniform soaked in blood. Later with his voice breaking frequently, Robert Parrish told the police, "In my opinion, Mack died so that I would get a chance." The sergeant, who was in charge of the canine unit, explained that Mack and the police officer were very close. "They lived and did everything together," he said. Then he added, "If it hadn't been the dog, it would have been the officer."

I suspect that every dog lover in my audience tonight knows exactly how Robert Parrish felt when Mack died. But, whether it is a story about a man and his dog, or about two friends, or about two brothers, one of the most beautiful themes, one of the most lovely subjects in all of human life and experience is the subject of partnership, companionship, and loyalty.

I would like to confront you with what I really believe is one of the most exciting truths in the entire New Testament. The truth is this: you and I are invited into partnership with the Son of God.

Now, please notice what I did not say. I did not say, that we are invited into the family of God. I did not say, that we are invited to possess eternal life. Of course, it is wonderfully true that, "God so loved the world that He gave His only begotten Son, that whosoever believeth in Him should not perish but have everlasting life" (John 3:16). Jesus, as we learned, "when He had by Himself purged our sins" (Heb 1:3c). So that by one simple act of faith in Him, we can possess eternal life and we can be members of the family of God. We can be perfectly, completely sure that we will live forever with God. But, I'm not talking about that right now. I am talking about partnership and companionship with Jesus Christ, God's Son.

Now, I suspect that every parent in my audience tonight will admit that one of your main concerns for your children is their companions. Particularly when your children reach teen years, you are very concerned that they have the right kind of companions, the kind who will not lead them astray, but who will be good for them. There is probably not a parent living, who has not at some time or other wished that they could choose their children's companions. It makes sense that when God the Father chooses companions for His Son, that He would wish to choose the best He could find.

Maybe we might suspect that in choosing companions for His Son, God would choose the angels. After all, where could God find better companions for His Son than in the angels? But, here is a surprise. The angels are not the companions of Jesus Christ.

In Heb 1:8, the writer reminds us that when God brings His firstborn back into the world, when Jesus returns in power and in glory, all of the angels of God will worship Him. We are informed that they are the servants of God. He makes His angels into spirits and ministers, His servants, a flame of fire (Heb 1:7). The angels worship and serve. But, there is a great gulf fixed between the role of the angels and the role of the Son. For while the angels worship and serve, the Son rules forever and forever.

Drawing upon the lovely words of Ps 45:6, the writer brings before us the very words of God to His Son. God speaking to Jesus Christ and saying, "Your throne, O God, is forever and ever; a scepter of righteousness is the scepter of Your kingdom" (Heb 1:8). What splendid words! What amazing words! God is speaking to Jesus Christ and calling Him God, promising to Him a throne that will last forever, and putting in His hands a scepter with which He will rule righteously. That is truly amazing.

One of the most beautiful pieces of music that has ever come from the heart and mind of man, it seems to me, is that oratorio which we know as Handel's Messiah.

The most famous part of Handel's Messiah is undoubtedly the Halleluiah Chorus. So noble and so majestic is the Halleluiah Chorus, that audiences rise to their feet. It begins as "Halleluiah, Halleluiah, the Lord God omnipotent reigneth". After a series of descending notes, we hear "the kingdoms of this world are become" and suddenly upward, "the kingdoms of our Lord, and of His Christ, and He shall reign forever and ever." Over and over again, the refrain is "He shall reign forever and ever."

I would like you to capture the vision of the future, which the writer of Hebrews puts before us. There is the Son, and He is God. He is sitting on a throne that is eternal, and He is ruling righteously. He is surrounded by the angels which are ten thousand times ten thousand, and thousands of thousands. They bow in adoring worship at His feet. They go forth from His throne to do His will like swift winds, like devouring fire. But, mark it well. The angels are not His companions.

In Heb 1:9, the writer continues with the words of Ps 45:7. God says to His Son,

> "You have loved righteousness and hated lawlessness; therefore God, Your God, has anointed You with the oil of gladness more than Your companions" (Heb 1:9).

You see, this King is not only God, He is also a man. When He was here on earth, He served God His heavenly Father perfectly. He loved righteousness perfectly. He hated lawlessness perfectly. Because of this, someday God will pour out upon Him like fragrant ointment, the surpassing experience of joy. "Therefore God, Your God, has anointed You with the oil of gladness more than Your companions" (Heb 1:9b). But, wait a minute. He has *companions* in His joy. Oh yes, His joy is greater than that of His companions and that is the way it ought to be. But, He does have companions.

You know, if you had been living in the ancient world, you would not have been surprised, even a little bit, to hear that a king should have companions. All kings in those days had companions. Do you remember that young man, Rehoboam, the son of Solomon? After the death of his father, he was about to ascend the throne, and he was waited on by a delegation from ten of the twelve tribes of Israel. They said to Rehoboam, "Look, your father Solomon was a tough king. He laid on us a heavy burden of labor and taxation. We would like you to relieve these burdens." Rehoboam said, "Let me think about it a little bit. Come back in three days and I'll give you my answer." So, the first thing Rehoboam did was to go to the old men, who had advised his father Solomon. He said to them, "What shall I give as an answer to these people?" The old men said,
"We think it would be very wise of you to grant their re-

quest. If you will deal gently with them on this occasion, they will be your servants forever" (cf. 1 Kgs 12:4-7).

Then Rehoboam went to the young men. The Bible says he went to the young men who had grown up with him. These were his companions. These were the men who were educated with the king. They were the men who looked forward to the day when their friend, the king, would come to power, because that would mean they would come to power, too. They expected to be his inner circle. Rehoboam said to these men, "What do you advise me to give as an answer to the people?" The young men said, "Hang tough. Stand firm. Don't give an inch, because if you give an inch, they will take a mile. Tell them that your father was tough, but you are going to be tougher. Lay down the law to them" (1 Kgs 12:8-11). That is what Rehoboam did.

It was not good advice, because it split the kingdom. But, these were his companions. These were the individuals to whom he was closest, and he listened to them. That was true of every king. Even in the Roman Empire, Caesar had his own inner circle who were called the friends of Caesar. They were often appointed to high positions in the kingdom. It was normal for an ancient king to have partners and companions in his kingship.

Now listen closely. The King about whom we are reading tonight does not find His partners among the angels. This King is a man and His partners are men. To put it very simply, every born-again Christian is invited into partnership with the King of Kings and Lord of Lords.

You say, "Zane, how do you know that? How can you be sure?"

Well, I know this from what we read later in the

book of Hebrews, "Therefore, holy brethren, partakers of the heavenly calling" (Heb 3:1).

Do you know that the word *partakers* in the original language is exactly the same word that we meet in Heb 1:9 and is translated *companions*? Therefore, we can translate Heb 3:1, "Therefore, holy brethren, *partakers* in the heavenly calling" as "Therefore, holy brethren, *companions* in the heavenly calling."

In Heb 12:28, at the very climax of the epistle, the writer says, "Therefore, since we are receiving a kingdom which cannot be shaken". What? Are we receiving a kingdom which cannot be shaken? Yes, we are. Why? Because Jesus Christ is receiving a kingdom which cannot be shaken. His throne is forever and ever, and because He is receiving that kingdom, so are we.

Can there be any such thing as a Christian, who listens to those words, who is not moved to the depths of his being? Think of it to be companions and partners with the King. Do you realize that in this auditorium, there could be a couple hundred kings and queens? I do not know how to count an audience, maybe there are three hundred, four hundred here. Is that not amazing? To be Partners of the King.

Well, you say, "Zane, what is the catch? There has got to be a catch somewhere."

Well, I have to confess there is what might be described as a catch.

In Heb 3:14, we read these words, "For we have become *partakers* of Christ". There is that word again. The word that is translated *companions* in Heb 1:9. "For we have become *companions* [partakers] of Christ, if we hold the beginning of our confidence steadfast to the end (Heb 3:14, emphasis added).

You see as we were saying earlier, the book of Hebrews was written to Christians who were tempted to give up. They were tempted to stop going to church and stop assembling themselves together. They were tempted to turn their back on their Christian faith and on their commitment to God and Jesus Christ. The writer of Hebrews says, "Please do not do that." If you cast away your Christian confidence, you will be throwing away your partnership with the King. We have become partners with Christ, *if* we hold the beginning of our confidence steadfast to the end.

In January 1981, President Ronald Reagan had just been inaugurated and he was busy filling all the positions in his new administration. Do you know that during those days, I was not hovering over the telephone waiting for a call from Washington, inviting me to participate in the Reagan administration? Ronald Reagan does not know Zane Hodges from a hole in the wall. Even if he did, I do not think he would appoint me to anything, because I have never worked for Ronald Reagan.

If you are talking about James Baker, Edwin Meese, Michael Deaver, or William P. Clark, then you are talking about people who have offices in the White House, who have positions of responsibility in the administration. The reason they do is because they knew Ronald Reagan before he became President, and they worked for him. But, I will confess something else. When Reagan did not call, I did not shed any tears.

You know, if Reagan is re-elected next year his administration will only last for eight years. I am just not interested in a position in a government that is only going to last eight years. You know what I am interested in? I am interested in a kingdom that cannot be shaken. I am interested in a post in a government that will go on and on and on, forever.

You know what I hope? I hope that when Jesus Christ comes back in all of His power and glory and sets up His eternal throne on this earth, I hope He will have a post in His government for Zane Hodges.

But, I will admit something to you. I am not absolutely sure about that. Now, do not misunderstand me. I am absolutely sure that I am a Christian. I am absolutely sure that I possess eternal life and that I will live forever in the presence of Jesus Christ. But, partnership with Jesus Christ is something you have to hold on to.

I am His partner right now. In fact, at this very moment, I am working for the future King right up here on this podium. But, I have got to keep on working right to the end. You see, it was Jesus who said in Rev 2:26-27,

> And he who overcomes, and keeps My works to the end, to him I will give power over the nations—'He shall rule them with a rod of iron; They shall be dashed to pieces like the potter's vessels'—as I also have received from My Father.

"The overcomer", says Jesus, "will rule the nations like I rule them."

In Rev 3:21, Jesus said, "To him who overcomes I will grant to sit with Me on My throne, as I also overcame and sat down with My Father on His throne." In other words, "I am My Father's partner in His throne, and the victorious Christian will be My partner in Mine." It was Paul who said, "If we endure, we shall also reign with Him" (2 Tim 2:12).

Dear Christian friend, if you are Christian by faith in the Lord Jesus Christ, you will always possess eternal Life. You can be absolutely sure of living forever with Jesus Christ. But partnership with the King is something that you have to hold on to. For we have become partakers, partners, and companions of Christ, if we hold fast the beginning of our confidence firm to the end.

There is a very lovely story about a young woman in the state of Maine, who was in love with a sailor. One night, as she and her boyfriend were together and he was preparing to sail away the next day, she made a promise to him. She promised that every night while he was gone, until he returned, she would put a light in her window. The next morning, her sailor friend got on board his ship and sailed away, and was never heard from again. Do you know what that woman did? She put a light in her window every night for fifty years until the day she died. That is loyalty. That is commitment.

My Christian friends, our Lord Jesus Christ has left the world, but it is only temporary. His Father has said to Him, "Sit at My right hand, till I make Your enemies Your footstool" (Heb 1:13). Someday, He is coming back to set up His kingdom and triumph over His enemies. His partners in that day will be those who have been faithful to Him and who have kept His works to the end. To put it very simply, the partners of the King are those who have kept their lights burning.

The songwriter was right, when he wrote "Give me oil in my lamp. Keep me burning. Give me oil in my lamp. I pray. Give me oil in my lamp. Keep me burning. Keep me burning 'till the break of day." Christian friend, if your light is always burning for Jesus Christ, you will always be a partner of the King.

> Therefore, since we are receiving a kingdom which cannot be shaken, let us have grace, by which we may serve God acceptably with reverence and godly fear (Heb 12:28).

CHAPTER 3

Suffering for the World to Come

READ: HEBREWS 2:5-10, 11-13, 18; 12:1-2

Jerry Garrison was a real problem child. At the age of about ten or eleven, he was a streetwise kid growing up in Sacramento. He really knew how to disrupt a classroom when he attended school. Probably, his poor behavior was not too surprising. His mother had died as an alcoholic. His father had been in and out of trouble with the law for years and is currently serving a term in prison for assault. He will not be eligible for parole until 1989.

One day about two years ago, Jerry and his brother Danny were visiting their father in a Sacramento apartment building. Jerry went into a vacant apartment to retrieve a toy that his brother had tossed inside. When he got inside the apartment, he heard a hissing sound. He went over to the gas stove and the valve was open. He could smell the fumes escaping. Instinctively, he started to run, but it was too late. There was a huge explosion. Jerry leaped over a couch, and he crashed through a window. He fell to the ground below, partly on the pavement and partly on the lawn. He was on fire. He got up and went over to a damp part of the lawn and began to roll around to put out the flames. His father put out the fire in Jerry's hair. Now this tough little kid was faced with the toughest battle of his entire life. Ninety percent of his body was covered with burns and doctors gave him only a ten percent chance to live.

One day, as he hovered near death in the burn ward of a Sacramento hospital, he was visited by his school principal, a man by the name Tom Dunlap. When the visit was over and the principal turned to go, Jerry said, "Mr. Dunlap, do you know something?" Mr. Dunlap said "What?" Jerry replied, "That's the first time that I ever looked you in the eye. I love you." Well, Mr. Dunlap knew what that was all about. He had disciplined Jerry many times at school, had looked him in the eye, and Jerry had always looked away. Now, this tough little kid was not only learning to look his principal in the eye, he was learning to face life and look it in the eye.

You would not be surprised to discover that Jerry beat the odds. He lived. But after he got of the hospital, his face was disfigured by the accident. His skin was white and puffy, his lower eyelids were red, and his mouth and nose were somewhat deformed. When he goes to school, he has to wear a sterilized silicon mask over his face to protect his skin. There are holes for his eyes and nose and slit for his mouth. The mask is held in place by a hood that fits tightly over his head. Other parts of his body are also swabbed in bandages. Lots of kids would not like to go to school that way. But, this gritty little kid, he is looking forward to the future. Doctors believe that surgery will be able to restore his face to normal by the time he's about sixteen years of age. Meanwhile, Jerry can take the occasional guff and ridicule for the way that he looks. "People laugh at me sometimes," he said, "they shouldn't be so rude, yet I'm getting used to it."[1]

Now, I do not know about you but, I think that is a pretty challenging story. I think that Jerry Garrison is a pretty brave, courageous, gritty little boy. Do you know what is wrong with lots and lots of Christians who are in the Christian church today? They do not have the courage and the grit that Jerry has. They are too soft and flabby. I am not talking about physical flab. (I am in no position to talk about physical flab.) I am talking about moral and spiritual softness and flabbiness.

Oh yes! It is easy to be upbeat when everything is going smoothly. We really can be gung-ho about our Christian faith when all the family is helping, when we are paying all of our bills, and when everything down at work is going smoothly. But, let things get tough, let them get hard, let them get frustrating and disappointing. Then, what kind of people are we?

I would like to tell you something that I want you to remember for a long, long time. It is this. "The world of the future belongs to those who endure in suffering."

You see, the writer of the book of Hebrews has been talking about the future world. He has been talking about that splendid day, when Jesus Christ will sit on a throne that will never end. After all of His enemies will

---
[1] *The Gadsden Times*, Gadsden, AL, November 14, 1982.

have been made the footstool of His feet, he is talking about the time when Jesus will be surrounded by His companions, who share in the joy of His kingship. There is one thing that the writer wants us to be sure to understand. He wants us to understand that the world of the future does not belong to the angels. He tells us in Heb 2:5, "For He has not put the world to come, of which we speak, in subjection to angels." The world to come does not belong to the angels.

You know, when I was a little boy, we would sing a song in which the angels were involved, that went something like this,

> Holy, Holy, Holy is what the angels sing. And I expect to help them make the courts of heaven ring. But when we sing redemption's story, they must fold their wings. For angels never felt the joy that my salvation brings.

That is true, is it not? Angels do not know the joy of being a sinner saved by grace. They do not know what it is like to receive the free gift of eternal life by faith in Jesus Christ. We know what that is about, but they do not. There is something else the angels do not know anything about. They do not know what it is like to suffer physically or to die. After all, the angels are a higher order of being. They are spirit beings, swift as wind and powerful as flames of fire. They do not have bodies of flesh and blood and bones like we have. In their experience, they know nothing about what it means to suffer physically or to die.

Here is something really, really amazing. God has put the world to come in subjection to creatures who are lower than the angels, and who know what it means to suffer. That is why the writer draws from the words of Ps 8:4-6,

> What is man that You are mindful of him, and the son of man that You visit him? For You have made him a little lower than the angels, and You have crowned him with glory and honor. You have made him to have dominion over the works of Your hands; You have put all things under his feet.

Would you like to feel really small and unimportant sometime? Hop in your car and drive out to the countryside. Can you do that in Los Angeles? Is there anything here but city? Well, presuming you can get out to the countryside and get out in a field or by a flowing stream some night. Stand there in the open and look up in the sky. Look at the moon, and all of its nighttime splendor. Look at the stars twinkling at distances so far away that we cannot even imagine how far they are. Then, think about yourself. I predict you will feel very small, insignificant, and unimportant.

That, I think, is the way the writer of the eighth Psalm felt one time,

> When I consider Your heavens, the work of Your fingers, the moon and the stars, which You have ordained, what is man that You are mindful of him, and the son of man that You visit him? For You have made him a little lower than the angels (Ps 8:3-5a).

But wonder of wonders,

and You have crowned him with glory and honor. You have made him to have dominion over the works of Your hands; You have put all things under his feet (Ps 8:5b-6).

Staggering thought!

Tiny man, living down here on this little ball, underneath the vast expanse of the universe. Tiny man, created to rule the creation. But, wait a minute. That is not the way it is. Go out to your own coastline and talk to the celebrities and wealthy people whose homes were destroyed by the fierce storms that lashed the West Coast earlier this year. Ask them, if man has control over the works of God's hands. They will tell you he does not. Go to Louisiana, to the areas that were under floodwaters earlier this spring. Ask them, if man has control over the works of God's hands. They will tell you that he does not. Oh yes, there are lots of things that man can control, but there are lots of things in creation over which he has no control.

But the writer of Hebrews tells us that when God says that He has put "all things under his feet", he means exactly what he has said. He means "all things." "But", says the writer of Hebrews, "we do not yet see all things put under him" (Heb 2:8). Man is not yet over the works of God's hands.

Last March, Gail Watson, a Dallas Texan, was in her kitchen one Sunday morning at about 10:45 a.m. She heard a tremendous crash. She rushed out of her kitchen, and she found a Pontiac Grand Prix that had crashed through the den, the dining area, and stopped in the living room about 20 feet from the kitchen. Fortunately, her two children were in another part of the house.

There was a man still sitting in the driver's seat. She went up to him and asked him if he was all right. He nodded that he was.

Then she started screaming. The impact finally hit her. The accident had happened as the Pontiac was heading north at a fast rate of speed on Rolling Rock Lane. It had skidded around the curb. It had crashed through a twelve-foot stretch of wooden fence and had gone another fifteen feet. It had crashed through the den and the dining area. When it came to a stop, the windshield was in the living room. The man who was driving it was arrested for driving without a license, driving without insurance, and reckless damage to property.

When he was released on bail later that day, he came to get some belongings out of the car, which happened to be a rental car. He said, "I sure indeed fell asleep and drove through it. It was an accident. What can I say?" Well, I suspect that Mrs. Watson would say that it would have been a good idea if he had stayed awake and kept control of the car. After all, people who drive cars are supposed to control the vehicles that they drive.

Man was made to control the creation, but the creation had crashed. It was a calamitous, tragic, resounding crash. Man had lost control of this world by his sin, by his fall in the Garden of Eden. He is not in control at all. We do not yet see all things put under him, but there is hope. For although we do not yet see all things under him, there is something we do see. We do see Jesus. We see Jesus who was made lower than the angels that He might taste death for every man. We see Jesus who, because He suffered, is crowned with glory and honor. He sits at the right hand of the throne of God expecting dominion over the entire world.

But, there is more. You see, God is in the process of bringing many sons to the glory of that dominion. Jesus is the Son of Man, and God is bringing many sons to share His dominion. In order to bring them to that glory, Jesus became a man and He suffered. He became their leader. That is why it is stated in Heb 2:10,

> For it was fitting for Him, for whom are all things and by whom are all things, in bringing many sons to glory, to make the captain of their salvation perfect through sufferings.

Because Jesus suffered, He is just exactly the kind of a leader that we need to lead us to that glory.

Colonel William Travis was the officer in command of the troops who were to defend the Alamo against the attack of the five thousand Mexican troops under the leadership of General Santa Anna. As the battle was approaching, Colonel Travis addressed his men, drew his sword, and drew a line in front of him. He said anybody who wants to escape is free to go. But anyone who wants to stay and die in defense of the Alamo, they will need cross that line.

The famous Davy Crockett was the first man across the line. The others followed him until there was only one man on the other side of the line. That was James Bowie for whom the Bowie knife was named. He was too sick to move under his own power, but he requested that someone carry him across the line and they did it. When everybody was across the line, Colonel Travis sent that brave message to General Santa Anna. He said, "We refuse to surrender."

On March 6, 1838, the attack began. It took three

waves of assault to overpower the defenders of the Alamo. Finally, they succumbed to the sheer mass of the numbers who were attacking them. When it was all over and everyone was dead, news of their bravery leaked back to the Army under the command of General Sam Houston. It was General Sam Houston who raised that famous cry, "Victory is certain! Remember the Alamo!"

I can assure you that in Texas, we do remember the Alamo. We remember it as a monument to human bravery and courage. But it is well to remember, that the key to that courage, lay in a brave leader, who had the capacity to inspire his followers, join with them in battle and die with them who defended that fortress.

My Christian friends, we have a great leader. Jesus was made lower than the angels. He became one with us in all respects. He shares our humanity. He shares our flesh and blood. He shares our experience of suffering and even the experience of death. For that reason, and this is wonderful, He is not ashamed to call us His brethren and declare His Father's name to us. Here is the bottom line. "For in that He Himself has suffered, being tempted, He is able to aid those who are tempted" (Heb 2:18).

My Christian friend, we are saved freely by the grace of God through faith in Jesus Christ. But, the road to glory and dominion over the creation is a tough road. We often encounter on that road, trouble, hardship, frustration and suffering. But, our Leader has traveled the road ahead of us. He has been victorious over everything. He has now sat down at the right hand of the Majesty on high. From there, He is able not only to help us, but also to inspire us.

That is why there comes ringing to our ears the challenge of Heb 12:1c, "Let us run with endurance the race that is set before us." Doing what? Heb 12:2,

> Looking unto Jesus, author and the finisher of our faith, who for the joy that was set before Him endured the cross, despising the shame, and has sat down at the right hand of the throne of God.

If that does not inspire you, nothing will.

Maybe some of you read the story of Phan Khan Trang in your newspapers not long ago. He is an eighteen-year-old Vietnamese teenager who decided he wanted to escape Communist dominated Vietnam. His goal was to come to California, where he has a sister living in Rosemead. Last April, he got aboard a ship with three relatives and nine neighbors, and they set out across the South China Sea. After three days, they ran out of food and water. On April 18th the ship was struck by a wave that Phan Khan Trang described as being as high as a house. The ship was shattered. Everyone had drowned except Phan Khan Trang, who somehow managed to get a hold of a plastic water container. For two days, he clung to that plastic water jug in the South China Sea until he was sighted by a Norwegian freighter, which picked him up and took him to Manila. Hopefully, he is with his sister today in Rosemead.

Now, that is a story about endurance. The ship shattered. His companions drowned. He was clinging to the only object that could keep him afloat.

The Bible is perfectly honest with us, my friends. The Bible does not promise us that our journey to the shores of the kingdom of God will always be across calm and passive seas. Often, violent storms sweep down upon us. The waves of trouble lash at our lives. We must cling to the only object that can keep us afloat. We must cling to our great Captain and Leader, whose help and whose inspiration can see us through to victory. For as surely as He was victorious, we can be victorious too. For you see, the world of the future belongs to those who have loyalty to Jesus Christ, and who endure in suffering because the Bible says, "If we endure, we shall also reign with Him" (2 Tim 2:12).

Just before I close, I would like to introduce you to Tale Venture. He was a poodle, and he belonged to Herbert and Audrey Harris, who live in Dallas. Unfortunately, last September, Tale Venture died of kidney failure at the ripe old dog-age of fifteen years. Herbert and Audrey were grief stricken. They wanted to do something that would memorialize Tale Venture. Now, Mr. Harris happens to be a wealthy real-estate investor. He called the Dallas Society for the Prevention of Cruelty to Animals (SPCA) to find out what they needed, and they told him. So, he wrote out two fifteen-thousand dollar checks just like that and promised more if it was needed.

The folks there established at the Dallas SPCA kennels, the Tale Venture Grooming Room, which offers free hair care to stray mongrels and other assorted dogs. You ask, what need does the SPCA have of a grooming room? Well, they had more need than you might think and the dogs had more need than you might think. You see, about fifty percent of the dogs who passed through the kennels find new homes and new and loving owners, but about fifty percent of them do not. They have to be led down to a back room and put to sleep. Sometimes, they are too old. Sometimes, they are too ugly to be adopted. Other times, the kennels are so crowded that they just have to make a hard choice. A dog's chance of finding a new home and escaping that walk to the back room improves greatly if he is well groomed.

Just to show you, during one two-week period, one-hundred eleven dogs were groomed at the Tale Venture Grooming Room and within two days, ninety of them were adopted. Mr. Harris commented, "Tale Venture lived a full life. Now he's going to be responsible for about 2,000 being groomed. I think he would be very proud." You know, I really liked the sentence with which that newspaper story opened. This is what it said, "Tale Venture died that other dogs might live and look sharp."

Now, I know that is a very pale and distant comparison. But allow me, will you? Jesus Christ came into the world, and died, not only that we might live with Him forever, but also that we might look sharp. If you will allow me to say it this way, this present life with all of its troubles, frustrations, and sufferings is our grooming room. For it is here that God prepares us for our future in His kingdom. It is here that He grooms us for our role in the government of the world and in the glory of dominion over the creation. Well do we sing at times, "Must I be carried to the skies on flowery beds of ease, while others fought to win the prize, and sailed through bloody seas? No, I must fight, if I would gain. Increase my courage, Lord! I'll bear the toil, endure the pain, supported by Thy Word."[2]

Make no mistake about it. The world of the future belongs to those who endure in suffering.

---
[2] Isaac Watts, "Am I a Solider of the Cross" (1721).

CHAPTER 4

Entering God's Rest

READ: DEUTERONOMY 12:8-10;
HEBREWS 3:7-19; 4:9-11

I would like to give you some sensitivity training. To begin with, I would like to introduce you to a remarkable woman who rates very high on the sensitivity scale. Her name is Alice Nelson Canon. She is an eighty-one year old woman who lives in Salt Lake City, Utah. One day last April, she and her husband decided to travel to St. George, which is in the southwestern portion of the state. If they had had the slightest idea how their trip would turn out, I am sure that they would never have left home. As they were traveling toward St. George, they decided to take a side trip into the Dixie National Forest and on one of the muddy roads in that forest, their car was mired down in an isolated section known as Pine Valley. It was April 15th. They spent the next two nights sleeping in the car, hoping, I suppose, that the roads would dry up or somebody would come by. On the morning of April 17th, they decided to try to walk out of the area.

But eventually they became tired and decided to build themselves a lean-to with sagebrush and pine branches. They slept that night under their lean-to. The night turned bitterly cold, and Mr. Canon died in his sleep. When Mrs. Canon woke up the next morning, she got up and she went on. At last, she came to a deserted summer cabin. She broke into the cabin and for the next four days, she lived off the canned fruits that had been stored in the cabin until at last rescue workers found her and took her to safety. By Saturday, after surgery, she was resting comfortably in the hospital.

Her relatives said that Mrs. Canon deeply regretted that she had to break into somebody's cabin. In fact, anticipating that she would die, she had actually left a note of apology, which read something like this, "I am sorry that I had to break into your home. It prolonged my life. My husband is dead lying out by some rocks not far from here." She promised to pay for the food that she had eaten. Then her note added, "Please call our children. They will be so worried. Thank you. Our children will remember you."

You know what? I think I would have liked to meet Alice Nelson Canon. My hat is off to an eighty-one year old woman who had the energy and determination to press on after her husband had died. But, that is not the thing that impresses me the most. The thing that impresses me the most about this woman is her remarkable and amazing sensitivity. Caught up in an ordeal, lost in the woods, deprived of her lifetime companion, and facing possible death herself, she is sensitive enough to write a note of apology to the people whose cabin she had broken into and whose food she had eaten.

My Christian friends, I want you to understand that in the Christian life, one of the greatest assets that you can possibly have is a sensitive heart. One of the surest signs of spiritual danger down the road is loss of spiritual sensitivity. The wise man of old said, "Keep your heart with all diligence, for out of it spring the issues of life" (Prov 4:23).

It is with good reason, therefore, that the writer of Hebrews drawing upon his vast store of OT knowledge, chooses as his text for this portion of his epistle (Heb 3:7-11) the ringing challenge of Psalm 95, "Today, if you will hear His voice: 'Do not harden your hearts, as in the rebellion'" (Ps 95:7b-8a).

It is out of deep pastoral wisdom and concern that he writes, "Beware brethren" (Heb 3:12). Did you notice that word, *brethren*? This is a warning addressed to Christians. "Beware, brethren, lest there be in any of you an evil heart of unbelief in departing from the living God" (Heb 3:12).

You see, deep down in the inner recesses and in the dark corners of our heart there lies the potential for doubting God. There lies the latent capacity for unbelief. If there is anybody, who would claim that you are never ever tempted to doubt God under any circumstances whatsoever, will you come forward after the meeting and introduce yourself? I will give you a charter membership in the liars' club of America. Let us be honest. We are capable. We are capable of doubting God. It is particularly under the pressures of stress and trouble that the latent capacity tends to rise to the surface, to seep into our hearts like some poisonous anesthetic robbing us of our spiritual sensitivity and hardening our hearts.

I was in Topeka, Kansas earlier this year. We have three very fine seminary graduates who are serving the Lord at a church there. It was my privilege to minister the word in that city. One night, after one of the meetings, we were in the home of one of these graduates. We went down into the basement for some refreshments and somebody said, "You know, it's good to be living in a city that has basements in the houses." Then they told me something about the city of Dallas that I had not realized before. They said, "You know, the reason they don't build cellars in the city of Dallas is because the soil is so rocky and so hard that it is too expensive to construct a cellar when you're constructing a house."

Now, Topeka needs its basements because, you see, occasionally a twister spins its way through the city of Topeka. In fact, one had passed through about a week before I came. When a twister is on the loose in the city about the safest place to be is in a cellar. Listen, my friends. If our hearts become hard, rocky, resistant soil, we have got no place to hide. We are sitting ducks for the twisters that sweep through our lives and experiences.

There is a danger that under those circumstances with hearts hardened by the deceitfulness of sin, that we may lose an inheritance of tremendous value and of tremendous worth. After all, it has happened before. You see, when God brought the children of Israel out of the land of Egypt and performed before their eyes all of those great signs and wonders, He led them to the very borders of the land of Canaan, the land of promise. Then, you remember, the children of Israel sent twelve spies into the land of Canaan to look the land over. Ten of those spies came back with a very discouraging report. They admitted that it was an excellent land that they had looked at. But they said, "The people who dwell in the land are strong; the cities are fortified and very large; moreover we saw the descendants of Anak there" (Num 13:28).

> "All the people whom we saw in it are men of great stature. There we saw the giants (the descendants of Anak came from the giants); and we were like as grasshoppers in our own sight" (Num 13:32c-33).

Forgive me if I suspect the Jewish spies of exaggerating a little bit and more than a little bit. Do you know how tall a man would have to be to make another man look like a grasshopper by comparison? I did a little calculating on this. Even if the Israelites were only on an average of five feet tall, their enemies would have to be 300 feet tall to make them look like grasshoppers. I really do not think that any of the people in the land of Canaan were much taller than Magic Johnson or Kareem Abdul Jabbar. But to hear the Jewish spies tell it, they were way up there and we were way down here. All they needed to do was to take their foot and stomp on us and they would crush us like a bunch of bugs.

Did you ever do that? I mean did you ever exaggerate your troubles just a wee little bit? Oh, my troubles are so big. I will never solve that problem. I will never lick that habit. I will never get through that difficulty. They weigh me down and crush me like a mere insect.

Oh, how hard the other two spies Joshua and Caleb tried to get the children of Israel to trust God. They gave a very eloquent speech. They said,

> "The land we passed through to spy out is an

exceedingly good land. If the Lord delights in us, then He will bring us into this land and give it to us, 'a land which flows with milk and honey.' Only do not rebel against the Lord, nor fear the people of the land, for they are our bread; their protection has departed from them, and the Lord is with us. Do not fear them" (Num 14:7b-9).

What an eloquent speech. "Don't get scared", said Joshua and Caleb. "These people are our meat. We'll eat them up. They have nothing to protect themselves. The Lord is with us." Marvelous! Courageous! Would you believe it?

When the children of Israel heard that speech, do you know what they thought about doing? Do you know what they talked about doing? They talked about stoning Joshua and Caleb to death. They said,

"These guys are trying to get us killed. They're gonna lead us into a land of giants. They're gonna wipe us out like a pack of sheep and slaughter us like so many pigs. Let's stone Joshua and Caleb."

That, my friends, is exactly what we mean by an "evil heart of unbelief in departing from the living God" (Heb 3:12).

Can you blame God for being angry with a nation like that? Can you blame Him for swearing in His wrath that they would never enter into His rest? The Word of God, drawing upon that incident so long ago, comes ringing down through the ages to you and to me. "Today, if you will hear His voice, 'Do not harden your heart, as in the rebellion'" (Heb 3:7b-8a). For you see, if we do, we may lose our inheritance and our rest as the Israelites also did.

I was reading, not long ago, about a hotel in the city of Tokyo called Luokani, that has a very unique way of helping its guests to rest. They have discovered that among the most restful sounds in all of the world are birdcalls. Would you believe it? They have a record with nothing on it but birdcalls. If a guest requests it, they will pipe birdcalls into their room, so they can relax and go to sleep. I am not talking about a birdcall to rest. I am talking about a Bible call to rest. I am talking about the most lovely invitation to rest that you can possibly conceive of, that is God inviting us to share His rest.

Will you not agree with me that in the English language, there are very few words that are more beautiful than rest? Here we are in the middle of July. Try to think about the hottest job you can perform in the city of Los Angeles. If you were living in Dallas, it might be getting out on a late Saturday morning and mowing your lawn. There you are pushing the lawn mower around the yard while the temperature rises steadily in the direction of 100 degrees. Sweat is rolling down your face. Your clothes are soaked. Finally after about two hours, you look out over that lawn and it is perfectly mowed and perfectly edged. Then you go inside your air-conditioned living room or your air-conditioned den. You sit down in your recliner, and you pick up a tall glass of cool lemonade. You turn on the television, and you sip your lemonade. That is rest and it is lovely.

As Jackie Gleason might say, "How sweet it is." But, did you know that God invites you into a rest that is even sweeter than that? Thousands of years ago, God worked for six straight days (Genesis 1). He worked and finally on the sixth day, He created man. He set man in control of all of the works of His hands, all of the creation. Then, what did God do? You know what God did. On the seventh day, He rested (Gen 2:2-3).

For a while, man shared that rest with God. But then, he blew it. He reached out his hand for the fruit of the tree of the knowledge of good and evil. He fell and he was expelled from the Garden of Eden, and vanished from God's rest (Genesis 3).

Now, the only way for man to get back into rest is by working for it. Now, I can just hear someone say, "Uh oh, Zane. Argh, he's gone and done it. Now, you're telling us that we have to work to get to heaven? Just wait until our Pastor gets up on the platform. He'll set that straight in no time flat." That is not what I am telling you.

The Bible is very clear on this subject, "For by grace, you have been saved through faith, and that not of yourselves; it is the gift of God, not of works, lest anyone should boast" (Eph 2:8-9). Paul wrote, "But to him who does not work but believes on Him who justifies the ungodly, his faith is accounted for righteousness" (Rom 4:5).

I hope that everybody in this audience understands that you can be saved and go to heaven freely by the grace of God. You can be justified, fully accepted before God by a simple act of personal faith in Jesus Christ, who died for your sins, and rose again. I hope we are clear about that. But mark it well, you will never enter this kind of rest unless you work for it.

Please remember that at the very beginning of my message, we read from Deuteronomy 12. The children of Israel are once again at the borders of the land of Canaan. They are about to enter into the Promise Land. It is clear from that passage that the word "rest" is used in the same way as the word "inheritance." Therefore, when we are talking about entering into God's "rest", we are talking about entering into our "inheritance." Now, do not forget what we have learned already from the book of Hebrews. Jesus Christ has sat down at the right of the Majesty on High. God has said to Him, "Sit at My right hand, Till I make Your enemies Your footstool" (Heb 1:13).

It is God's intention and purpose to give to the Lord Jesus Christ dominion over all the world, dominion over the creation. But as we have seen, God is also bringing many sons to share the glory of His kingship, His authority, and His dominion with Him. The King has companions. He has partners. To enter into this partnership is to enter into our inheritance and into our rest.

C. H. Spurgeon, the famous preacher, once preached to an audience in excess of twenty-three thousand people in a place called the Crystal Palace. That was on a Wednesday. When he came home, he went to bed on Wednesday night, and he slept until Friday morning. All day Thursday, his wife looked in on him, and she found her husband sleeping peacefully and wisely decided not to disturb him.

Now, I can empathize with that. You folks out there, that have never been up on a platform and preached, let me tell you something. Preaching is work. It is draining, emotionally, physically, and psychologically. Some mornings when I am finished with my Sunday morning sermon at Victor Street Bible Chapel in Dallas, I head straight back for my apartment and for my bedroom. Now, I have to admit to you, that I have never preached to twenty-three thousand people. Therefore, I have never slept twenty-four hours after a sermon. But, I can just imagine how draining this was for C. H. Spurgeon. He had done a special work for God, and God had given him a special kind of rest.

For those who work for God right up to the end, God has a special kind of rest. That is why we read in Heb 4:9-10, "There remains therefore a rest for the people of God. For he who has entered His rest has himself also ceased from his works as God did from His." God labored for six days. When He finished, He rested. For those who labor for God, when their work is finished, they will rest.

Now, please do not misunderstand me. I am not suggesting that we are going to sleep for ten thousand years in the Kingdom. That would get very old, very fast, and we would miss an awful lot of action. No. God calls us to a rest that is better than sleep. He calls us to a rest that is better than sitting in our recliner and sipping lemonade. He is calling us to an experience of rest that is better than anything that we have ever called "rest". He is calling us to the rest of sitting down in the experience of kingship with Jesus Christ our Lord.

Jesus said, "To him who overcomes I will grant to sit with Me on My throne, as I also overcame and sat down with My Father on His throne" (Rev 3:21). When the struggles of life are over, when the battles are fought and won, when our job for God is finished, God will say to you and to me, "Sit down, My son." "Sit down, My daughter." "Sit as a king." "Sit as a queen." "This is My Sabbath rest. For now, man has dominion again over the creation in the person of Jesus Christ, My beloved Son." This is our rest and this is our inheritance.

This is the reason, that the writer of Hebrews challenges us by saying, "Let us therefore be diligent to enter that rest, lest anyone fall according the same example of disobedience" (Heb 4:11). This is a rest that can be missed. The Israelites in the OT, through hardness of heart and through unbelief, did not enter in.

If our hearts remain sensitive to God and to His Word, if we continue to trust God to enable us to conquer the giants and to capture the fortified cities of our life, if we trust Him to help get the job done, we will enter that rest. We will obtain that inheritance.

Four years after the sinking of the Titanic, a great disaster in which 1,500 lives were lost, a young Scotsman got up in a meeting in Hamilton, Canada. He told this impressive story. He said,

> "I am a survivor of the Titanic. On that awful night, I was floating in the ocean, clinging to a spar from the wreckage of the ship, when the waves brought to me Mr. John Harper of Glasgow who was also clinging to a piece of wreckage. As we came close to each other, Mr. Harper said to me, 'Man, are you saved?' And I said, 'No, I am not.' Then Mr. Harper said, 'Believe on the Lord Jesus Christ and thou shall be saved.'"

Then, said the young man,

> "The waves parted us. But, strangely enough, after a while, the waves brought him back to me. And he said, 'Are you saved yet?' And I said, 'No, I can't say that I am.' And he said to me, 'Believe on the Lord Jesus Christ, and thou

shall be saved.'

"Shortly after that, John Harper went down. He went under. That night, under the darkened sky, with two miles of water beneath me, I believed. I am John Harper's last convert."

Thrilling story, caught in a famous disaster, John Harper clinging to a piece of wreckage for his very life, remained sensitive to the spiritual need of another human being and sensitive to his responsibility to God. He bore witness to the saving power of the name of Jesus and He served and worked for his Master until the last moment of His life. Who was he? He was one of the heirs. He was one of those who entered into rest. He was one of the partners of the King.

CHAPTER 5

Saving the Saved

―――※―――

READ: PSALM 3:5-8; 110:1-4;
HEBREWS 1:13-14; 4:14-16; 5:5-10; 7:24-25

Dick Cockrell is a real live flesh and blood hero. In 1980, he was a truck driver for Kroger stores. He was at an East Texas roadside park one day, when he saw three men trying to drag a woman and her two young daughters into a car. The woman was screaming for help. There were about 8 or 10 bystanders in the area who were doing nothing to save her. That is when Dick Cockrell moved into action. Now, to understand what happened next, you have to know that Dick Cockrell is an ex-Marine. He is five foot, eleven inches tall, and he weighs about 245 pounds. He is a very husky fellow. He has had more than the normal experience with thugs and bullies. In fact, he grew up right here in the Los Angeles area.

When he was a teenager, he was overweight. He

weighed over 300 pounds. He took a lot of abuse because he was fat. So, he joined the Marines, quit school, and got into shape. When he would come back on leave from the Marines, he would spend his time looking up the bullies, who had made his life miserable, evening up the score with them.

So, Dick Cockrell knew what he was doing when he waded into these three men, even though one of them was holding a knife. Very quickly, and efficiently, he broke one man's jaw, he broke another man's arm, and he disabled the third man with a very well placed kick. As the men lay writhing on the ground in pain, he told them that he passed that way three times a week and if they would like more of the same, they could hang around and he would be sure to give it to them. Well, it was all in a day's work for Dick Cockrell, and he did not even bother to tell his employer what had happened.

But the woman's grateful husband telephoned the Dallas Times Herald and told them the story. The wire services picked it up and spread it all over the nation. Pretty soon, Dick Cockrell was being flooded with congratulatory telephone calls, cards, and letters. The phone lines at Kroger were so tied up that the supervisor said it looked like he was going to have to hire an answering service just to handle Cockrell's calls.

Cockrell told the Dallas Times Herald that he was a little surprised that he had not received more crank calls than he did. He said he just got one. A fellow who said he was with the Ku Klux Klan called to say that they were gonna get him for helping that black woman. Cockrell said, "I didn't tell them that the three guys who were attacking her were also black." Well, he was a hero. But, he told the media that all the reward that he wanted was what he got shortly after the fight was over. When the two little girls, ages six and seven, hugged and kissed him, Cockrell said, "That made my day."

Well, I am sure that it did. But, I am sure of something else as well. It also made the day for that woman and those two little girls who were saved from their attackers. I would like to suggest to you that the situation of Christians in this world is very similar to the situation of that woman and those two little girls. You see, we also are under attack.

Oh, I know that in this country, that does not usually come in direct physical form. Yet, we should never forget that there are Christians all over the world who are in literal, physical, danger because of their Christian faith. But for us, the attacks come sometimes in more subtle ways. The attacks may come in terms of personal rejection, in terms of ridicule, hostility, or hatred. Above and beyond all of these things are the unceasing attacks that come from the enemy of our souls, from Satan himself. Strange as it may seem when you first hear it, we who are saved need to be saved.

Many centuries ago, King David was driven from his palace and driven from Jerusalem by a rebellion that was started by his very own son, Absalom. You will remember that Absalom was an exceedingly handsome young man. From the crown of his head to the sole of his feet, he looked every inch a king (2 Sam 14:25). He was also a very crafty fellow and he managed to steal the loyalty of the twelve tribes of Israel, so that they wanted him for their king, and rejected David who had ruled them so long and so well (2 Samuel 15). David had to flee from Jerusalem with a small group of loyal servants and a small band of dedicated soldiers.

David had not gotten very far from the city of Jerusalem when he got very alarming news. David got word that Absalom was mobilizing the entire army of Israel and was about to lead them out to attack David and his men, with the intention of slaughtering David's men and killing David, Absalom's father (2 Samuel 16-17). Many brave men might be excused for being a little worried in a situation like that. David might have said "This is it. We are hopelessly outnumbered. We have no place to go. We have insufficient supplies. This is the end." He might have said something like that but he did not.

Did you know what David did when he got that news? He got a good night's sleep. In Ps 3:5-8a, which was written about that very occasion, David says,

> I lay down and slept; I awoke, for the Lord sustained me. I will not be afraid of ten thousands of people who have set themselves together against me all around. Arise, O Lord; Save me, O my God! For You have struck all my enemies on the cheekbone; You have broken the teeth of the ungodly. Salvation belongs to the Lord.

Did you hear those words? David says, "I know I am outnumbered, that they are setting themselves against me all around. But, God has punched my enemies in the mouth and knocked their teeth out. Salvation belongs to the Lord." You know what happened, do you not? When the battle was joined between David's tiny band of men and Absalom's huge army, it was Absalom's men who were routed and not David's (2 Samuel 18). It was Absalom who was killed in battle and not King David because salvation belongs to the Lord.

My Christian friends, do you know what we need when we are under attack? We need someone to save us. We need someone who is strong enough to punch our enemies in the mouth and knock their teeth out. That is exactly what we have in Jesus Christ. Through Him, we can inherit salvation.

I was talking to a young woman some years ago, trying to explain how to be saved. I told her the Bible said, "Believe on the Lord Jesus Christ, and you will be saved" (Acts 16:31). I explained that because He died for her sins and rose again, all she needed to do to be saved from hell was to believe Him as her personal Savior. Then I said to her, "Have you ever done that?" She said to me, "Yes, I have." I was a little surprised by that. "Oh", I said, "when did you do that?" She told me about an occasion when she had been driving a car. She had been involved in an accident. As I remember it, she said there was serious damage to both cars. The police arrived and she was very afraid that she was going to get into trouble. So she said, "I asked the Lord to save me. He did and I did not get into trouble."

When she told me that, I knew that we were talking about two different kinds of salvation. I was talking about salvation from hell and eternal judgment, and she was talking about salvation from trouble. Of course, the Bible does talk about salvation from eternal judgment. Jesus said,

> "Most assuredly, I say to you, he who hears My word and believes in Him who sent Me has everlasting life, and shall not come into judgment, but has passed from death into life" (John 5:24).

But, there is another kind of salvation that the Bible also talks about very often. Over and over again in the book of Psalms, not only in Psalm 3 but in many other Psalms, the writers cry out to God for salvation from their enemies, for deliverance and victory in the midst of troubles. Their theme is "salvation belongs to the Lord."

Do you know that is exactly the kind of salvation that you and I can inherit? Why can we inherit that kind of salvation? It is because God has said to His Son, "Sit at My right hand, till I make Your enemies Your footstool" (Heb 1:13). Jesus will be victorious over all of his enemies. Through Him, we can be victorious too. As He sits on that throne of victory, the angels are sent out as ministering spirits to serve those who shall inherit salvation, who shall share His victory (Heb 1:13-14).

Napoleon Bonaparte was undoubtedly one of the great military geniuses of all time. At the peak of his career, as emperor of France, he brought practically all of Europe to its knees. Then Napoleon decided to invade Russia. Napoleon's Russian campaign must certainly go down as one of the great military disasters of all time.

I have read that, in the city of Wilna, on the border of Russia, there is a simple granite shaft. On the western face of that shaft, the direction from which Napoleon invaded Russia, there are inscribed these words, "Napoleon Bonaparte passed this way in 1812 with 410,000 men." On the eastern face of the shaft, from which direction Napoleon retreated from Russia, are these words, "Napoleon Bonaparte passed this way in 1812 with 9,000 men." You see the great military genius and commander, though he was, he led literally hundreds of thousands of men to disaster and to defeat.

You cannot follow Jesus Christ to defeat. It just cannot be done. I hope you remember what we are learning from the book of Hebrews—that God designs to bring many sons to the glory of dominion over the entire creation. He has provided for those many sons a Captain of their salvation who is perfect for His role. He can lead them to victory. But, there is a condition.

In Heb 5:9, we read these words, "And having been perfected, He became the author of eternal salvation to all those who obey Him."

Is everybody awake? I mean, is everybody in this audience wide-awake? Was there anybody in the audience, who heard those words read or quoted, who thought that the verse was talking about being saved from hell by obeying Jesus Christ? If you did, go to the foot of the class. Shame on you, if you thought that these words were talking about eternal judgment. Maybe in some churches we could understand a mistake like that, but not in this church.

Do you not agree? Do we not all understand here that the Bible says, "not by works of righteousness which we have done, but according to His mercy He saved us" (Titus 3:5a)? Do we not remember that the Apostle Paul wrote, "But to him who does not work but believes on Him who justifies the ungodly, his faith is accounted for righteousness" (Rom 4:5)? If you thought Heb 5:9 was talking about salvation from hell, you really needed to pay closer attention to the verses that are right in front of it. Heb 5:7-8, speaking of Jesus Christ,

> who in the days of His flesh, when He had offered up prayers and supplications, with vehement cries and tears to Him who was able to save Him from death, and was heard because

of His godly fear, though He was a Son, yet He learned obedience through the things which He suffered.

Come with me, to one of the most touching scenes in all of the Bible. Come to the garden of Gethsemane. There is Jesus with three of His most intimate disciples, and He knows that in a very short time, his enemies will appear. They will arrest Him and lead Him off to suffering and death. He turns to Peter, James, and John and He says, "Watch and pray" (Matt 26:41) while I go over there and pray. Jesus goes off a little bit. The Bible tells us that He fell on his face and from the depths of His heart, He prayed, "O My Father, if it is possible, let this cup pass from Me; nevertheless, not as I will, but as You will" (Matt 26:39). Three times, He prayed that prayer (Matt 26:42, 44).

I think it is just about enough to bring tears to our eyes when we realize that the Bible says that He prayed out of the anguish of His heart, that the sweat that rolled down His forehead was like great drops of blood falling to the ground (Luke 22:44). Do you know what happened in the garden of Gethsemane? Jesus learned obedience. That cup was not taken away. God's will was done. Pretty soon, the enemies arrived led by the traitor Judas who planted that kiss of treachery on Jesus' cheek. Then they bound Him, and they led Him through a series of trials that made a mockery of justice. They nailed Him to a cross like a common criminal. As He hung dying on the cross, He offered up prayers and supplication to God with strong crying and tears.

If you want to know what He prayed on the cross, you only need to turn to Psalm 22, which begins with that cry of desolation,

> My God, My God, why have You forsaken Me? Why are You so far from helping Me, and from the words of My groaning? O My God, I cry in the daytime, but You do not hear; and in the night season, and am not silent (Ps 22:1-2).

For twenty-one verses, that anguish prayer goes on. But, here is how it ends, "But You, O Lord, do not be far from Me; O My strength, hasten to help Me! Deliver Me from the sword, My precious life from the power of the dog. Save Me from the lion's mouth and from the horns of the wild oxen!" (Ps 22:19-21a). The very next words of that Psalm are thrilling. Do you know what they are? The very next words of the Psalm are these, "You have answered Me" (Ps 22:21b). Jesus, "who, in the days of His flesh, when He had offered up prayers and supplications, with vehement cries and tears to Him who was able to save Him from death, and was heard because of His godly fear" (Heb 5:7). He was heard "because of His godly fear."

How did God hear him? First of all, He raised Him from the dead;

> Up from the grave He arose with a mighty triumph over His foes; He arose a victor from the dark domain and He lives forever with His saints to reign ... Hallelujah, Christ arose.[1]

But, that was only the first step, because He had learned obedience, because He had become obedient unto death, even the death of the cross.

---
[1] Robert Lowry, "Up from the Grave, He Arose" (1874).

> Therefore God also has highly exalted Him and given Him the name which is above every name, that at the name of Jesus every knee should bow… and that every tongue shall confess that Jesus Christ is Lord, to the glory of God the Father (Phil 2:9-11).

"Sit at My right hand, till I make Your enemies Your footstool" (Ps 110:1). Is that not amazing? I mean, is that not wonderful? Jesus obeyed God and God gave Him eternal salvation. Jesus obeyed God and God gave Him eternal salvation delivering Him out of all of His troubles and out of the sufferings of death, exalting Him to the highest place in the universe, and giving Him victory and dominion forever. Eternal is this deliverance.

My friends, if we are willing to obey Him, we too can share in that same eternal salvation. We too can be victoriously triumphant in the midst of life's troubles and we can share in His eternal reign. But, we need His help. We really and truly need His help. In the very same Psalm where God says to His Son, "Sit at My right hand, till I make Your enemies Your footstool" (Ps 110:1), God says something else to Jesus that is very important for every Christian in this audience tonight. For in Ps 110:4, God also says to His Son, "The Lord has sworn and will not relent, 'You are a priest forever according to the order of Melchizedek.'" The reason that we can make it in the Christian life is because in Jesus Christ, we have a great high priest.

I was reading some time ago about a Vietnam veteran by the name of George Faulkner. He bears the scars of his wartime experience. He has a nervous condition, a skin disease, and ulcers. He and his family of four were in a third story hotel room one time in Jellico, Tennessee. The hotel caught on fire, and the flames were so intense that it was impossible to go to safety through the hallway. He and his family went to the window of their third story room.

George Faulkner jumped out and landed on the roof of a one-story building that was right up against the hotel about 15 or 20 feet below. Then his wife brought their six-month-old little daughter, Susan, to the window. She threw her out the window and George Faulkner caught her. Then, their 4-year-old little boy, George, climbed up in the window and he jumped out of the window. George Faulkner caught him and broke his fall. He landed safely. Then his wife, Maggie, also jumped and George Faulkner caught her and broke her fall. She landed safely. As if that were not enough, three more times, he went back into the hotel trying to save people until he had taken in so much smoke, inhaled so much, that he could not go back in anymore. A hero? You better believe it. In time of crisis, he saved his entire family.

Christian friends, what we need in times of crisis, is someone into whose arms we can leap. We need someone who is strong enough to catch us, to break the fall, and to see to it that we land on our feet. We need a veteran. We need someone, who knows the pathway of suffering and has paid the price of obedience to God. All of that we have in Jesus, our great High Priest. Therefore, the writer tells us in one of the most beautiful passages in the book of Hebrews,

> Seeing then that we have a great High Priest who has passed through the heavens, Jesus the Son of God, let us hold fast our confession.

> For we do not have a High Priest who cannot sympathize with our weaknesses, but was in all points tempted as we are, yet without sin. Let us therefore come boldly to the throne of grace, that we may obtain mercy and find grace to help in time of need (Heb 4:14-16).

I would be lying to you, if I told you that the Christian life is easy. It is easy to be saved from hell, but it is not easy to live victoriously for God. But, it is my privilege to announce to you, to proclaim to you, that the throne of victory on which Jesus is seated is also a throne of grace. When we come to God in prayer, through Jesus, we can get everything we need to be victorious. That is why the writer tells us, in Heb 7:24-25a,

> But He, because He continues forever, has an unchangeable priesthood. Therefore He is able to save to the uttermost [save completely] those who come to God through Him.

Why? Because He is always alive to pray for His people. He forever lives to make intercession for them. If we are talking about salvation from our troubles, from our trials, or from our enemies, whether human or demonic, He can get the job done. He can get it done. He can save us completely. He can save us to the uttermost.

> When I fear, my faith may fail,
> Christ will hold me fast.
> When the tempter would prevail;
> He can hold me fast.
>
> He will hold me fast,

He will hold me fast;
For My Savior loves me so,
He will hold me fast.[2]

Salvation belongs to Jesus Christ our Lord.

During World War II in the North African Campaign, the German troops were led by a shrewd and capable General Rommel. He earned the title, "The Desert Fox." Time after time, he inflicted defeats on Britain's army in North Africa. Finally, Britain sent to North Africa to take command of their defeated and demoralized troops, Field Marshall Bernard Montgomery. After Montgomery had been there for a little while, he turned to General Lord Ismay, who was a general under his command. Montgomery said to Lord Ismay, "You know, it seems very sad to me that a professional soldier can reach the very peak of his generalship and then suffer a reverse that ruins his career." Lord Ismay responded, "Don't be depressed. Maybe, maybe you will win through." Montgomery replied, "My dear fellow, I was not talking about myself. I was talking about Rommel."

Students of World War II will tell you that this confident commander reorganized the British troops, and lead them to victory over Rommel, "The Desert Fox." I think that it ought to thrill us right down to our bootstraps, that the Captain of our salvation is a confident commander. For Him, victory is sure. If we are willing to trust and obey Him, we can be victorious too.

I think that what I have tried to say to you can be summarized in the simple words of a little chorus, which

---

[2] Ada Habershon, "He will Hold me Fast" (1906).

goes like this,

> My Lord knows the way through the wilderness. All I have to do is follow. My Lord knows the way through the wilderness. All I have to do is follow. Strength for today is mine always. And all that I need for tomorrow. My Lord knows the way through the wilderness. All I have to do is follow."[3]

---

[3] Sidney E. Cox, "My Lord Knows the Way Thru the Wilderness" (1951).

CHAPTER 6

The Peril of Not Growing

READ: HEBREWS 5:12-14; 6:4-8, 11-12

It probably will not come as a surprise to most of you, but when I was a little boy, I sometimes disobeyed my mother. Like most little boys who disobey their mothers, I was frequently tanned on the seat of my education. But, there was one occasion when I disobeyed my mom, when she treated me like an angel in disguise.

We were living, at the time, in a second floor apartment in a place that we called Beechwood. I was about three or four years old. My brother, David, was about one year old. He was still in his crib. Something that I did displeased my mother, and she banished me to the living room and told me not to go back into the bedroom without permission. Well, that was still a long time before they invented TV, so I got very bored in the living room.

So, I decided to sneak back into the bedroom without my mother noticing me. But when I got back in, I got a shock. My brother had athletic talents, and he was obviously developing them early. His crib was sitting next to some French windows, one section of which was open. Believe it or not, he had climbed up out of his crib. He climbed through the open section of the windows probably knocking a screen out in the process. He was standing outside of the windows, on the windowsill, holding on to the section of the windows that was closed. There was a sloping roof behind him and if he had lost his balance, he probably would have rolled down the roof and fallen onto the ground. Now, I do not remember doing this, I grabbed David's clothes, but my mother assures me that I did. But, I do remember screaming at the top of my lungs for mother to come here quick. When she got there, she was horrified. She snatched David back into the room, put him in his crib, and closed the French windows.

Do you suppose that I got rebuked for going back into the bedroom without permission? No way. With one stroke, I had been transformed from a disobedient brat into a family hero. Maybe, just maybe, I saved my brother's life.

Now, no parent in this audience is going to be surprised at all, by a story like that. Every parent knows that as soon as a baby gets the power of locomotion they have a strong tendency to crawl, toddle, or walk wherever their little heart desires. They can get themselves into the most awful of predicaments.

In fact, when you really stop to think about it, babyhood, infancy, is just about the most dangerous period of our lives. Do you realize that it is exactly the same in Christian life? One of the most dangerous periods in our entire Christian life and experience is the time when we are babies in the family of God, when we are babes in Christ.

Back at Victor Street Bible Chapel, where I preach the word on a regular basis, we really love the birthday song. In particular, we like the second stanza. "Happy birthday to you, only one will not do. Born again means salvation. How many have you?" If you are the one being sung to, you are supposed to hold up two fingers to indicate that you have two birthdays; one, the birthday in which you were born into this world physically, and the second, the birthday on which you were born into the family of God by faith in Jesus Christ, the day that you received eternal life through personal faith in our Savior.

You know, for some people, the interval between those two birthdays is a long, long time. No matter what age you are saved at, after you get saved, you are a baby in the family of God. Even if a man is sixty, seventy or eighty years old—and he looks very experienced and mature from a human point of view—if he has just gotten saved, he is just a babe in Christ. You know that is perfectly normal, that is perfectly natural. The problem comes if we remain a baby too long.

I happen to think that one of the great tragedies in the Christian church today, is that there are so many Christians who have been saved for years and years and they have barely grown at all in the Lord. They are still babies.

You know what would be kind of a funny and sad thing to be able to do in an audience like this? Suppose I had a magic wand that I could wave out over the audience, and every Christian would be transformed into the physical side that corresponds to your development in Christ. Boy! We would look around at the audience, and we would be laughing our heads off at some people. Some of us might have very red faces. You know, there might be grown up people who would be reduced to the size of a little baby in diapers? Adults would shrink to the size of a little six-year old girl or an eight-year old boy. There might be some of you who will look older than you do physically because you have grown and developed so well in Jesus Christ. But, when a person remains a baby too long, that is tragic. It is more than tragic. It is dangerous. It is very, very dangerous.

Apparently that was what was wrong with the Christians to whom the book of Hebrews was written. They had been Christians for a long time, and they had scarcely grown at all. The writer says to them,

> For though by this time you ought to be teachers, you need someone to teach you again the first principles of the oracles of God; and you have come to need milk and not solid food (Heb 5:12).

Everyone who only uses milk is unskillful in the word of righteousness because he is a baby. "Look here," says the writer of Hebrews, "you folks have been Christians long enough. You ought to be able to teach someone something about the great truths of the Christian faith. But it looks to me like you need to go back to grade school, go back to kindergarten. You need somebody to teach you the ABCs of the Christian faith. You can't take in the solid food, the deep truths of God's Word. You can only take in the simple things, the basic things, the milk." "And look", says the writer, "anybody who just uses milk is just a little baby unskilled in the word of righteousness."

There was a school principal, who was very disappointed, because he did not get a promotion that he had set his heart on. He was complaining to the superintendent of schools about it. He said to the superintendent, "After all, I've had twenty-five years experience." The superintendent replied, "No, Joe. That's where you're mistaken. You've had one year's experience twenty five times."

You know there are Christians like that. They are no further along today than they were at the end of their first year of Christianity. They have had one year's experience five times, ten times, twenty-five times. It is dangerous. Do you know why it is dangerous? It is because baby Christians cannot make the kinds of decisions that Christians need to make. They have a hard, hard time telling the difference between the things that are good for them, and the things that are bad for them.

Put a little baby out on the carpet of your living room. Let him crawl around a little bit. Then put in front of that little baby a brightly colored marble and a clear uncut diamond. The marble is worth maybe twenty-five cents. The diamond is worth thousands of dollars. The chances are very good that the baby is going to prefer the brightly colored marble. A baby does not know the difference between a marble and a diamond. He has no concept of the comparative value of these two things. He is likely to choose the thing that appeals to his baby senses.

That is precisely the danger that baby Christians face. They are "unskilled in the word of righteousness" (Heb 5:13). "But", says the writer of Hebrews, "solid food belongs to those who are of full age, that is, those who by reason of use have their senses exercised to discern good and evil" (Heb 5:14). Mature people know how to make the right choices. They choose the good. They refuse the evil.

Jimmy Breslin is fed up with kids, not just with other people's kids, with his own kids most of all. Now, just in case you do not know who Jimmy Breslin is, he is a kind of a celebrity, a playwright, a journalist, and a novelist. Sometime ago, he appeared on "Talk Show" with Charlie Rose, and they got onto the subject of kids. Jimmy Breslin was explaining that his wife had passed away about a year before and left him with a family of kids to raise. He had finally found out what kids were like. He said to Charlie Rose, "They are lousy. There's no sense in being nice about it. They don't stand up. They're selfish." Charlie Rose thought to himself, "This guy's putting me on", but pretty soon he realized that Breslin is serious.

So he starts to press him for examples of what he was talking about, and Breslin was happy to oblige. Breslin said, "All right. One day, I was sitting at home working on this important book. And I sent my sixteen-year old daughter to the supermarket. And she comes back with $150 worth of cake and cookies. And the kids are in the kitchen fighting over what she had brought back. So I go in and I say to her, 'Why did you bring all this stuff back?' And she says to me, 'Because that's all they had on the isle that I shopped tonight.'" So, Breslin says, "She goes to the supermarket, she shops on one isle, she brings back what they got, and the kids are fighting over it, and I kicked them out of the house. They're selfish. They haven't done one kind thing all year." Charlie Rose asked, "Nothing?" And Breslin said, "No, nothing. I'm not kidding you. You'll find out. They're lousy." Rose says, "Well, surely, surely they bring a lot to your life." Breslin says, "No. They don't bring anything. They bring you $150 worth of cake when you send them to the supermarket."

Now, when I hear a story like that, I do not know whether to laugh or cry. I do not know who is in worse shape, Jimmy Breslin's kids or Jimmy Breslin himself. But, one thing is obvious. That girl does not know how to shop in a supermarket.

Do you know that there are lots of Christians who do not know how to shop in the supermarket of life? You turn them loose in the supermarket of life, and they will head straight for the isle with the sweets on it. Do you know what I am talking about? The big, bright cars. The big, fancy houses. The expensive clothes. The costly vacations. The good things of life. That is what they choose. They choose the marbles of life and they turn their back on the diamonds. They do not know how to tell the difference between good and evil. They choose the things that hurt them, and they fail to choose the things that would benefit them and bring glory to the God of heaven. They sometimes choose poison.

Have you ever noticed how many manufacturers tell you to keep their products out of the reach of children? Just about all medicine bottles these days have these childproof caps that are hard for children to unscrew. They are a pain in the neck, because I cannot get the cap off myself sometimes. But, children have a strong tendency to put small things in their mouth without discriminating. They cannot tell the difference between food and poison. I think one of the things that really concerns the writer of Hebrews is that he is afraid that his readers may drink poison. He is afraid that these immature Christians, who can only drink in the milk of the word, may end up drinking in the poison of apostasy. He is afraid that under the pressure of circumstances, trials, and tests, they will be discouraged, and they will give up. They will throw their Christian faith overboard, and walk away from it.

Have you ever watched a bunch of kids playing? Maybe there is one kid in the bunch that just cannot do anything right. I mean, he cannot win for losing. Pretty soon they are going to see him get up and say, "I quit. I don't want to play this old game anyway. I'm gonna go home." He picks up his marbles or whatever he was playing with. He walks off, and he quits. Sometimes, when the game of life gets tough, sometimes when it is difficult to persevere in the pathway of obedience to God, a Christian, particularly an immature Christian, may say, "I quit. I don't need this Christianity bit anyway. I was better off like I was before."

That is exactly why the writer of Hebrews, over and over again, warns his readers to hold firm to their Christian commitment. "Let us hold fast the confession of our hope without wavering" (Heb 10:23a). It is precisely because he is afraid that some of his readers may waver. In Heb 6:4-6, he pens words that must certainly go down as among the most solemn words in the Word of God. The writer says,

> For it is impossible for those who were once enlightened, and have tasted the heavenly gift, and have become partakers of the Holy Spirit, and have tasted the good word of God and the powers of the age to come, if they fall away, [it is

impossible] to renew them again to repentance, since they crucify again for themselves the Son of God, and put Him to an open shame (Heb 6:4-6).

I want you to know that these words of solemn warning come very close to home for me. You see, I have a friend, and more than a friend, a man who labored with me side by side in the ministry of God's Word in the little group that has become Victor Street Bible Chapel. This friend has fallen away from the Christian faith. He came from overseas and when he got over to this country, he married a very fine Christian girl. He graduated from Bob Jones University and from Dallas Theological Seminary.

About the time when he and his wife left Dallas, his wife contracted a very serious illness, which over the years got progressively worse until she was reduced to being a complete invalid. After the death of his wife, I visited my friend who now lives in the Midwest and who teaches ancient history at a secular university. As we sat in the living room together, face-to-face, he told me very frankly but graciously, that he no longer claimed to be a Christian at all—that he no longer believed the things that he had once preached and taught.

The situation was even worse than he described because I heard through others that in the classroom on the university campus, he often mocked and ridiculed the Christian faith. As I sat in that living room, I was very painfully aware that it was impossible for me to talk that man into changing his mind. It was impossible for me to talk him back to the convictions that he had once held. It was impossible for me to renew him to repentance. You want to find someone harder to deal with than an unsaved person? Find a person like that.

The writer of Hebrews tells us that "it is impossible", after a man has been spiritually "enlightened," after he has received the priceless "heavenly gift," after he has actually become a "partaker of the Holy Spirit," and "tasted" the goodness of the "Word of God" and the power of Christianity, which is "the powers of the age to come," it is impossible to "renew" such a one to "repentance". Because you see, what they are doing is just the same as putting Jesus Christ back on the cross. They are rejecting Him as He was rejected so long ago. They are putting Him to an open shame.

I am going to tell you something. I do not like to talk about my friend's story. I virtually never talk about it unless it is in a message like this, because I am ashamed of this. Oh, how disgraceful for a man to have known the truth, to have proclaimed the truth, and then to deny the truth. He has put the Son of God to an open shame.

Well, one may be thinking, "I guess he's headed for hell, right? I guess he's headed for eternal damnation. He's renounced his Christian faith." Wait a minute. I did not say that. Neither does the writer of Hebrews. Let me remind you that Jesus said, "I am the bread of life. He who comes to Me shall never hunger, and he who believes in Me shall never thirst" (John 6:35). Jesus also said,

> "the one who comes to Me I will by no means cast out. For I have come down from heaven, not to do My own will, but the will of Him who sent Me. This is the will of the Father who sent Me, that of all that He has given Me I should

lose nothing, but should raise it up at the last day" (John 6:37b-39).

We have Jesus' word for it that if a man comes to Him for the bread of life, He will never need that bread again. He will never under any circumstances be cast out because Jesus is determined to do the will of God. God's will is that He lose no one. He has never lost anyone, and He never will. I grieve because my friend and brother has lost his faith, but Christ has not lost him.

Do you believe in the grace of God? But hold it. I do not want anybody to say to themselves, "Well, I guess it doesn't really matter what we do after we're saved, huh? Throw your faith away, mock Christianity, still go to heaven. It doesn't really matter what you do." Oh, yes it does. My friend is safe from the fires of hell. But, he is not safe from the righteous anger of God. He is not safe from the fire of God's chastisement, discipline, and retribution. He lives in the shadow of disaster.

That is why, in Heb 6:7-8 the writer speaks words that are both very encouraging and terribly threatening. The writer says,

> For the earth which drinks in the rain that often comes often upon it, and bears herbs useful for those by whom it is cultivated, receives blessing from God; but if it produces thorns and briers, it is rejected and near to being cursed, whose end is to be burned (Heb 6:7-8).

Have you ever been out in the country, driving through the countryside and you saw a field on fire? I come from Pennsylvania, from farm country, and I have seen it. You may at first think, "Well, the fire started accidentally." But, as you get closer to the field, you notice that the fire is under supervision. Maybe the field has real tall grass on it and it has lots of weeds. It becomes evident that the owner of the field has set fire to his own field to burn off the grass and weeds. This agricultural practice was known way back in the days of the Bible. The purpose of burning a field was not to destroy the field but to destroy the rank and unacceptable growth that the field had produced.

When we become a Christian, we are a lot like a plot of ground that belongs to God. God has poured out upon us the blessings of His grace like rain from heaven. He has a right to expect that our lives will be fruitful, productive, and useful to men. When they are, He blesses that life. But, if after the rain has fallen upon our life, if after we have received the blessing of His matchless grace, we produce briars and thorns, the fruits of a sin cursed world, then God rejects that kind of a life. It falls under His temporal curse. Its destiny is to suffer the fire of His discipline, His chastisement, and His retribution.

I happen to think that the reason why it is impossible for us to talk an apostate Christian back to his former convictions is because God reserves that individual for the fire. If recovery in this life is ever to happen, it will only happen after the individual has passed through the searing reality of God's righteous retribution. I know that is heavy, but the writer of this epistle is heavy.

In Hebrews chapter 10, where the writer is talking about the same thing, he says, "For we know Him who said, 'Vengeance is Mine, I will repay,' says the Lord. And again, 'The Lord will judge His people'" (Heb 10:30). Did you hear that? The Lord will judge, not the unsaved, not in this context. The Lord will judge *His people*. "It is a fearful thing to fall into the hands of the living God" (Heb 10:30). For our God is a consuming fire. "But," says the writer, "that's not the experience I want you folks to have. That's not what we desire for you. We desire that you should show the same diligence under the full assurance of hope unto the end, that you may not be sluggish. But that you may be growing, growing, growing. That you may be imitators of those who, through faith and endurance, inherit the promises. Hold on." The writer says, "Let us hold fast the confession of our hope without wavering, for He who promised is faithful" (Heb 11:23).

My dad has discovered one of the joys of retirement, which for him, is gardening. When I was up north in Pennsylvania, just a few weeks ago, I was given the special tour of his garden this summer. Everything was growing fine. You know, one of things we do not realize when we are looking at a garden is the tremendous powerful growth that is there.

Do you know what I have read? That turnip seeds, which I understand, are very tiny seeds. When they are in their growing season and under ideal conditions, they can increase their weight as much as fifteen times a minute. Under the very best of conditions, they can increase their weight fifteen thousand times a day.

There is nothing more powerful than a growing squash. This boggled my mind, but here is what I have read. An eighteen-day-old squash has been harnessed to a lever, and has been able to lift fifty pounds. If that does not surprise you, nineteen days later, the same plant harnessed to the same lever, was able to raise 5,000 pounds. It is the miracle of growth that God has imparted to tiny seeds with the capacity to grow like that.

You may feel like a very tiny and insignificant Christian. But, I am going to tell you this: The Holy Spirit of God lives in your heart. All of the power that God has is resident in every Christian. The miracle of growth can take place. There is no reason to remain a baby. There is no reason to fail. There is no reason to give up. "Therefore do not cast away your confidence, which has great reward" (Heb 10:35).

CHAPTER 7

The Secret of Success

※

READ: HEBREWS 10:19-25, 28-31, 35-38

When Jules Trop turned forty-five years of age, it looked like he had everything going for him.[1] He was a physician in Miami Beach. His medical practice brought him lots and lots of money. He owned a waterfront home on a private island in Biscayne Bay. He owned a prized art collection. But, he also had something else. He had cocaine. Many of his wealthy patients both used and sold cocaine. Eventually, Trop was drawn into the cocaine habit. "It made my conversation seem sparkly," he said. "It made music sound better. It made me feel good. In fact, it was sort of like drinking at a fountain of youth." He could now outrun his 19-year-old son in the 3-mile race. His sex

---
[1] "Fighting Cocaine's Grip: I Thought I Was God," *Time Magazine* (April 11, 1983).

life improved. "I became the macho man that I always dreamed of becoming."

After a little while, he was spending $1000 a week on cocaine, taking two grams, smoking two grams a day, and sometimes with only minutes between "toots." Even when he was driving in his car, he took a little sniff on his hand. After a year of cocaine use, he discovered free-basing. Now his social highs became highly anti-social. "In the beginning," he says, "I thought I was communicating with God. And at the end, I thought I was God."

With the help of an unsuspecting nurse, he somehow managed to maintain his medical practice. But at home, his life was coming unraveled. He was not disturbed by the constant small fires that he caused with his free-basing equipment. By this time, he was spending $2000 a day on cocaine. He only wanted to be alone, away from his disapproving wife and children. Eventually, he moved out of his mansion and moved into a dilapidated apartment. He says, "I was chasing the high, the memory of the high. But the highs got lower, and the lows got deeper."

Now, his skin was covered with sores and malnutrition. The free-basing caused rashes on his body, and his mouth was so swollen that he could hardly talk. Shards of broken glass stood in a pile in his apartment as high as his thigh. The apartment was rancid, filled with unwashed clothes and dishes. But the doctor did not notice. He was now spending most of his time in the shower, even smoking his coke in the shower to remove the constant sweating. He said, "I went as low as you can go without dying." The road back was tough. He had sold off his art collection, and he had mortgaged his home in order to pay for his habit. After going to a series of treatment clinics, he gradually began to rebuild his marriage and his career. But, even today, although it has been nearly three years since he had any cocaine, Jules Trop freely admits, "I am only a hit away from where I was before."

Unfortunately, the story that I have just told you, is not unique. There are many stories very much like it that you can read and hear today. I have not told you this story because I want to talk about America's drug problem, even though that problem is very serious and very real. I have told you the story because I am interested in something that is far broader and deeper than drugs. I am interested in man's tragic capacity to reach the highest level of personal experience, to fall from that level, and to plunge down, down, down into the depths of misery and ruin.

Perhaps more than any other book in the Bible, the book of Hebrews faces this tragic capacity in man. Even more to the point, it faces this capacity as it results even in true Christians. Even in those who come to know our Lord and Savior Jesus Christ.

Years ago, when I was still a student at Wheaton College, some of the other students at Wheaton used to go into Chicago on Sunday mornings to skid row to bear witness for Jesus Christ. I suppose that every major city has its own skid row, a street or a section of the city that is dominated by beer joints and flop houses. Populated by bums and winos, these dedicated young students would go into the city on Sunday morning to share the gospel of Jesus Christ with the derelicts, who lived on skid row. I shall never forget the reports that they brought back sometimes. They said that often, more than once, as they were witnessing to some bum or wino from the word of God, they would receive a response like this, "Yeah. I know all about that. I used to go to Sunday school. I used to go to church. I was saved, when I was a kid. But, I got away from all that and here I am today."

Now, I know that some of those who responded in that way probably were not Christians at all. But the tragedy is that probably some of them were. When the writer of the epistle of Hebrews reminds us that, "Anyone who has rejected Moses' law died without mercy on the testimony of two or three witnesses" (Heb 10:28), he then adds to that these solemn words,

> Of how much worse punishment, do you suppose, will he be thought worthy who has trampled the Son of God underfoot, counted the blood of the covenant by which he was sanctified a common thing, and insulted the Spirit of grace? (Heb 10:29).

When the writer of Hebrews writes like that, it reminds us of the solemn fact that there are some punishments that are worse than death. There are some experiences that are worse than execution.

Turn sometime to the book of Lamentations, read the grievous laments that fall from the lips of the daughter of Zion, as she looks out over the land of Judah, as she mourns for the tragedy that has fallen upon Judah, as they have come under the judgment of God. Listen to the cry of the prophet who says,

> The punishment of the iniquity of the daughter of my people is greater than the punishment of the sin of Sodom, which was overthrown in a moment, with no hand to help her! (Lam 4:6).

"Oh", to paraphrase the prophet, "I just wish that we could have been wiped off the face of the earth, like Sodom was. That would have been better. That would have been better than this. This is worse." There are punishments that are worse than death.

If the time ever comes when we turn our backs on the grace of God and the truth of God's Word, God does not have to kill us. God does not have to send us to hell to repay us. That is why the writer of Hebrews says,

> For we know Him who said, 'Vengeance is Mine, I will repay,' says the Lord. And again, 'The Lord will judge His people.' It is a fearful thing to fall into the hands of the living God (Heb 10:30-31).

You say, "Wow. This is a real down deep message." It is an honest one so far, because this is what the Word of God is telling us. But, I am happy to be able to tell you that there is no reason why you should fall into the hands of the living God. Because you see, it is our supreme privilege to fall at His feet. It is our privilege to fall at the feet of God in praise, gratitude, submission, surrender, and worship.

In Heb 10:19-25, before the writer ever speaks the grim and solemn words that we have been talking about in the last few minutes, the writer puts in the pages of his epistle one of the most eloquent passages in the entire letter. A passage that is rich with exhortation, with encouragement, and with hope. In Heb 10:19-25, it seems to me that we reach the very heart and core of what this writer desires from the depths of his heart for the experience of his readers.

I would like to suggest to you that in Heb 10:19-25, we have what might be called a divine antidote to apostasy. To put it another way, we have a divine prescription for spiritual victory. It all begins with boldness.

> Therefore, brethren, having boldness to enter the Holiest by the blood of Jesus, by a new and living way which He has consecrated for us, through the veil, that is, His flesh, and having a High Priest over the house of God, let us draw near with a true heart in full assurance of faith (Heb 10:19-22a).

You cannot be a successful Christian if you are a frightened Christian. You cannot be a victorious Christian if you are uncertain about the nature of your relationship to God and about the privilege of access that you have into His presence. The first element in remaining victorious is boldness.

There is a story that is told about Napoleon. On one occasion, Napoleon was riding a horse. He lost control of the horse, and the horse ran away with him. An ordinary soldier stepped right out of the ranks, a soldier we might describe as a buck private. He grabbed the reins of Napoleon's horse, and he pulled it to a stop. Napoleon looked down at the man, and he said, "Thank you, Captain. Thank you, Captain." The soldier realizing that he had just been promoted and without a moment's hesitation, responded, "Of what regiment, sir?" Napoleon replied, "Of my personal guard." That is boldness. Face to face with the emperor of France, relying completely on the emperor's words, he gained access to the personal presence of the emperor by becoming a member of his personal guard.

Do you realize that it is our high and holy privilege to come face to face with the Emperor of the universe, to come into the very presence of God at any time with prayer, with praise, and with worship? When Jesus hung on the cross, bearing that immense load of the guilt of your sins and mine in a wicked world, as hung in that dramatic darkness, something very remarkable happened. The veil at the temple, that thick curtain that kept men out of the holiest part of the Jewish temple, was torn. It was rend from top to bottom. In this symbolic act, God was signifying to men, that by the rending of the flesh of Christ on the cross, the way was now open into His presence. We have a new and living way through the veil, that is, through His flesh. Every moment, we can draw near to God with a full assurance of faith.

Queen Victoria is said to have had a strong tendency to visit the humble and the lowly. On one occasion, she was visiting an elderly woman who lived in a cottage all by herself. This woman happened to be a happy believer in Jesus Christ. As the queen got up to leave, she said to the woman, "I'd like to do something for you." The woman said, "Thank you, your Majesty, but I have everything that I need." The queen replied, "But, I really would like to do something for you." "Your Majesty, thank you," said the woman, "I have all I need, but maybe you could just promise me one thing." The queen said, "If I can do it, I will." The woman said, "O Majesty, would you please promise to meet me in heaven?" Very calmly and very firmly, Queen Victoria replied, "I shall do that by virtue of the blood of the Lord Jesus Christ."

It seems to me that, in that story, we reach the very

essence of true biblical Christianity. A humble cottage woman and a famous queen promising to meet each other on the shores of heaven and assured that they can do so, not because of what they have done or what they hope to do for God, but by virtue of the blood of Jesus Christ. That, my friends, is the basis of a true heart that approaches God with the full assurance of faith. One of the things that the writer of Hebrews wants us to understand truly is the greatness and sufficiency of the sacrifice that Jesus Christ made on the Cross.

In the longest expository section of this epistle, stretching all the way from Heb 7:1 to Heb 10:18, the writer has expounded for us the marvelous role and ministry of Jesus Christ. To Whom God has said, "The Lord has sworn and will not relent, You are a priest forever according to the order of Melchizedek" (Heb 7:21b). As the great High Priest in the order of Melchizedek, Jesus offered a sacrifice. Something that none of the sacrifices of the old covenant could do. "For it is not possible that the blood of bulls and goats could take away sins" (Heb 10:4).

But this Man, after He had offered one sacrifice for sin forever, sat down on the right hand of God, and expecting His enemies to be made the footstool of His feet. By one offering and this is wonderful, "For by one offering He has perfected forever those who are being sanctified" (Heb 10:14). Each and every believer in Jesus Christ, on the basis of the cross work of our Savior, has a standing before God that is perfect. You know that I can come to God at anytime. I can come as one whose heart is free of guilt, "sprinkled from an evil conscience." I can come to God as one whose body is "washed with pure water" (Heb 10:22). For He has washed me, sanctified me, and justified me. Therefore, I come confidently, I come boldly, and I come with assurance.

You know what really delights me? It is the realization that wherever I am on the face of the globe, I can walk instantly into the throne room of heaven. The first night that Luis, a friend, and I were in a hotel, as we were getting ready for bed, Luis said to me, "Zane, I think it would be nice, each night, before we go to bed, if we would read a passage of Scripture." So we sat down and read a passage of Scripture. When we were finished, Luis said, "Now, I think we should pray." He said, "I like to kneel when I pray." So, he got down on his knees at the foot of his bed, and I got down on my knees at the foot of my bed. We closed our eyes and began to pray. Do you know something? There is a sense in which we were no longer in the hotel, lovely and attractive as those accommodations were. We had stepped into the Holiest of all. Instead of bowing before a bed, we were bowing before the throne of grace. We were holding audience with the King of kings and Lord of lords. Does that thrill you? It should.

Here is the first ingredient in the divine prescription for victory. It can be summarized in four simple words. "Let us draw near." But there is a second element in the prescription. It also can be summarized in four simple words. "Let us hold fast." "Let us hold fast the confession of our hope without wavering" (Heb 10:23a). Let us hold onto it.

I want to suggest to you that the person, who is clinging fast in the present privilege of coming near to God for all his needs, will not find it all that difficult to hold on to his hope for the future. I trust that by this time, all of us have understood that the book of Hebrews is setting before us a hope that is more than simply to be with God, even though that is a very wonderful hope, indeed. For the book of Hebrews sets before us the marvelous privilege of sharing in the power and dominion of Jesus Christ in the world to come, the privilege of becoming partners with the King. That is the hope to which we are to cling. But there is one thing we have to be sure of. "Let us hold fast the confession of our hope without wavering, for He who promised is faithful" (Heb 10:23).

I was talking to you a moment ago about Queen Victoria, a very remarkable queen. She also had a very remarkable prime minister. His name was Lord Palmerston. It is said on one occasion that Lord Palmerston was walking across the Westminster Bridge. There was a little girl in front of him carrying a jug of milk, and she dropped the jug of milk. It shattered on the bridge. The milk was spilt, and the little girl dissolved into tears. The prime minister went up to her, wiped the tears away, and consoled her. But, because he did not have any money on him that day, he said to the little girl, "Look, if you'll come back to this bridge tomorrow at this time, I will pay you for the jug and the milk."

Well, the next morning, Lord Palmerston was in a cabinet meeting with the other ministers of state. All of a sudden, he remembered the little girl. He jumped up without explanation. He rushed out of the cabinet meeting leaving the startled ministers gaping and wondering where he had gone. He went back to the Westminster Bridge, and there was the little girl. He dropped a half-crown in her open palm. The little girl learned something about the prime minister that day. She learned that he who promised was faithful.

I think it is very lovely that along the Christian pathway, when we have frustrations, disappointments, and problems and it appears to us that we have dropped the jug, the milk has spilt, and we are inclined to dissolve in tears, it is lovely that there is Someone who draws alongside of us and comforts us, strengthens us, and wipes the tears away. But, I will tell you something else that is equally lovely. It is to hear the same person say, "I'm coming back. And when I come back, I will repay you for this." Whatever the frustration, whatever the problem, whatever the disappointment, if you endured in submission to Me, I will repay you when I come.

You know, my friends, I think it is possible that the readers of Hebrews had begun to wonder about the promise of the Lord's Coming. The writer has to tell them, "For you have need of endurance, so that after you have done the will of God, you may receive the promise: 'For yet a very little while, and He who is coming will come'" (Heb 10:36-37a). He who promised is faithful.

The songwriter has taught us to sing, "It will be worth it all, when we see Jesus. Life's trials will seem so small when we see Him. One glimpse of His dear face, all sorrow will erase. So bravely run the race till we see Christ."[2] "Let us hold fast the confession of our hope without wavering, for He who promised is faithful." (Heb 10:23)

Have you gotten these two parts of the formula? "Let us draw near" and "let us hold fast." But, there is one final element of the prescription. Frankly, it is a little bit surprising. The third element is, "Let us consider." Let us consider what or whom? This is the part that may sur-

---
[2] Esther Kerr Rusthoi, "When We See Christ" (1941).

prise us. Let us consider "one another." "Let us consider one another in order to stir up love and good works, not forsaking the assembling of ourselves together" (Heb 10:24-25a). Not giving up church. "But exhorting one another, and so much the more as you see the Day approaching" (Heb 10:25b).

I was in a man's home years ago. I was inviting him to church, and he said to me, "I really don't go to church. I can worship God, you know, out in the field, out by the lake. I don't need church." My, what a familiar refrain. I bet your pastor has heard it in every stanza and verse in which it can be sung. "I don't need to go to church because everybody at church is a hypocrite." "I don't need to go to church because the folks at church aren't friendly." "I don't need to go to church because I don't get anything out of it." "I don't need to go to church because _____." Fill in the blank. Fill in the blank with almost anything.

You know what is wrong with all of those excuses? They consider only ourselves. Try this on for size. "I'm going to church because my brothers and sisters down at church need me. They need my encouragement. They need my love. They need my concern. They need my exhortation. They need to have me help them while they help me along the road as we wait for the coming of our Lord Jesus Christ." Now that is a good reason for going to church. Do you know something? To try out that approach would be doing *yourself* one of the biggest favors you can possibly do.

You know the Bible says, "It is more blessed to give than to receive" (Acts 20:35c). The Bible says, "He who waters will also be watered himself" (Prov 11:25b). Jesus said, "For even the Son of Man did not come to be served, but to serve, and to give His life a ransom for many" (Mark 10:45). One of the best things you can do for yourself is to stop thinking so much about yourself, and to begin to think about others. Therefore, one of the secrets of spiritual victory is, "And let us consider one another in order to stir up to love and good works" (Heb 10:24).

Have you got the whole formula? It is easy to remember. "Let us draw near with boldness." "Let us hold fast without wavering." "Let us consider one another with loving expectation." That is the path to victory.

If you should ever happen to come to the city of Dallas, which I hope you will, let me recommend a restaurant to you. It is called Baby Doe's. It is laid out in a turn of the century mine setup. The story behind Baby Doe is an exceedingly interesting story. Baby Doe[3] was a beautiful divorcee when she met a man named Horace Tabor who was a wealthy miner. Mr. Tabor had made millions of dollars off of the mine which he called the Matchless Mine in Leadville, Colorado. Mr. Tabor divorced his wife and married Baby Doe. Their wedding was one of the great social events of the early West. The President of the United States was invited and he came.

But not long after the wedding, a series of reverses struck Mr. Tabor and he lost everything. He died heartbroken and poverty stricken. But just before he died, he gave a final word of admonition to Baby Doe. He said, "Have faith in the Matchless Mine. Don't give it up. It will repay you all that I have lost." Well, Baby Doe believed that promise and for the next thirty-six years of her life, as she became an aging widow, she lived close

---
[3] Real name was Elizabeth Bonduel McCourt Doe, 1855-1935.

to the Matchless Mine despite crushing adversity and repeated court orders designed to get rid of her. In 1935, in a dilapidated shack, close to the Matchless Mine, Baby Doe died nearly penniless because she had put her faith in a promise that could never be fulfilled.

Do you realize that the world in which we live is pock-marked with dry holes and worthless mines? The story of Baby Doe has been repeated a hundred different times by men and women of the world, who set their hope on something in this world which can never fulfill or reward them.

But, you know something? I could wish that in our spiritual lives we were all like Baby Doe. Because, you see, the Christian faith is the only "matchless mine" there is. It is from this mine that we dig the silver and gold of eternity. It is from this mine that we draw the riches of the world to come. It is from this mine that we can dig the splendid privilege of being a partner with the King. So, have faith in the matchless mine. Never give it up. Whatever it has cost you to be obedient to Christ will be doubly repaid when He comes again.

So,

> For you have need of endurance, so that after you have done the will of God, you may receive the promise, "For yet a very little while, and He who is coming will come and will not tarry" (Heb 10:36-37).

CHAPTER 8

The Journey of Faith

Read: Hebrews 11:1-2, 4-7

Most of you have probably seen Patricia Neal on television as she plugs for Anacin. As she tells her viewers in that raspy voice of hers, "Fight headache pain and win." Well, Patricia Neal is almost ideal for a commercial like that, because she has been fighting all kinds of pain for a long, long time. Of course, she is a very talented actress. She won a Broadway Tony for her role in "Another Part of the Forest." In 1964, she won an Oscar for her role in "Hud." But her life story reads like a bad television script. In 1953, she married a British writer named Roald Dahl. Seven years later, she was struggling with the rehabilitation of their young son, Theo, who had been struck by a New York taxi. Theo recovered but was left with mild brain damage. Later, the couple lost a daughter, Olivia, to the measles.

In 1965, Patricia Neal suffered a series of strokes that

left her comatose for two weeks and threatened to thoroughly destroy her powers of speech. Her husband stood by her faithfully. Pushed, prodded, and encouraged by him, she managed to recover sufficiently to give birth to their daughter, Lucy, who is now seventeen, and eventually, to resume her career in films and television. But the story does not have a happy ending.

About nine years ago, when she was doing a television commercial for Maxim Coffee, she met a wardrobe woman who soon became a family friend and a frequent houseguest. Unknown to Neal, she also became a rival for the love of her husband. In a particularly candid interview with People magazine, Patricia Neal described the situation.

She explained that the woman came from a fine home, had been married, and had three children. She said,

> "It's horrible to look back on how many times we were together on holidays, and I never knew. I even took her into my home for two weeks after she had been hospitalized. One time when she was at my house, we were having a girl talk. She was telling me about her new love, a married man who had one son, and three daughters. 'Oh', I said. That's just like Roald and me. Being her friend, I wanted happiness for her. So I said to her, 'Would your lover ever leave his wife for you?' 'He'd like to,' she said. 'He doesn't love her.' Of course, she was talking about Roald right to my face. And I didn't even know it. Oh, it was ghastly."

Indeed, it was ghastly.

About a year and a half after the affair began, Patricia Neal found out about it. She confronted her husband. He admitted it, but he gave her the impression that the affair was over, and she believed it. "I should have known better," she said. "But, I guess I didn't want to. I had loved him so many years. And, to me, when you are married, you are married forever."

Three years ago last December, she discovered the affair was still going on. It now was obvious that the marriage was ruined and Patricia Neal had come back to this country. Dahl had sued her for divorce. Speaking to *People* magazine, she said, "So many horrendous things have happened to me. But, the fact that our marriage has not worked is the most agonizing. I just can't swallow it. It is as if the worst dream I can think of has happened."

Now, the story of Patricia Neal is a classic case of trust betrayed. A husband, who one loves and trusts, proves to be unfaithful. A friend, who wanted help and was trusted, proves to be no friend at all. It has happened over and over again in human experience. No doubt, it will happen many times more.

But a story like this reminds us of a very basic and simple fact of life: All of our valuable relationships in life are built on trust. When a husband and wife stop trusting each other, they may continue to be married, but they can no longer have a happy marriage. When two friends stop trusting each other, they may continue to see each other, but, they no longer have a true friendship.

If that is true in our human relationships, how much more is it true in our relationship to God?

In one of the truly great statements of the Bible, the

writer of Hebrews tells us, "But without faith it is impossible to please Him" (Heb 11:6a). There is no way that our relationship with God can be pleasing to Him unless we trust Him.

Do I need to remind you that that is where it all begins for us? The way that we become a Christian in the first place is by an act of faith, by an act of trust. When I come to the living God as a guilty sinner who deserves to go to hell and when I receive from Him, through Jesus Christ, the free gift of eternal life, I am engaged in a tremendous act of faith. I have never seen God. I have never seen this place called heaven, or the place called hell. I have never seen Jesus Christ. I have never seen this thing called eternal life. Yet, when I believed God's Word, those things which I cannot see become reality to me. They take on substance for me. By faith, I gain assurance and conviction about things that my eyes cannot behold.

That is what faith is all about. The writer of Hebrews tells us, "Now faith is the substance of things hoped for, the evidence of things not seen" (Heb 11:1). By faith, we reach out and lay hold of realities that are invisible to our eyes. But getting saved is only the first step. It is the start of a journey that cannot be traveled successfully in any other way than by faith.

Now, I feel constrained to tell you about the way in which I recently earned my badge as the chicken of the sky. I was traveling to Topeka earlier in the year, in the month of May. I arrived in Kansas City by an American Airlines jet. I was supposed to travel from Kansas City to Topeka on a commuter service called Capital Air Service. When I got to the correct terminal and went up to the ticket counter, the ticket agent surprised me by asking me how much I weighed. Now, I have been flying the airlines a long time and no ticket agent has ever asked me how much I weighed before. But I was too naïve to figure it out, and so I sat down in the waiting room with two other people. I kept looking out the window for the Capital Air Service jet to arrive, and it never did.

After a while, an employee motioned for the three of us to follow him down some stairs and out on the landing strip. When we got out there, I realized why they had asked for my weight. We were not going to Topeka in a jet. We were going in a little tiny four-seater that had a seat for the pilot and a seat for each of the three passengers. I want you to know that I climbed aboard that plane with growing anxiety. My nervous system does little blips even when I go up the glass elevator to the top of Reunion Tower in Dallas. I could just imagine what blip-blops my nervous system was going to do bouncing along in the clouds in that little thing.

Then they started to load the baggage. They had a lot of baggage, and they were having trouble cramming it into the little tail section behind my feet. I happened to be carrying with me a big heavy box of Redención Viva books. I said to myself, "If the passengers and the rest of the baggage don't bring the plane down, the Redención Viva books surely will." It was then that my spine turned a sickly shade of yellow, and I announced to the surprised pilot that I had just decided not to go to Topeka on that particular flight. Would they give me my baggage back, please? By the time I got outside the terminal with my baggage, the same bus driver who had left me off a few minutes ago, picked me up again. He laughed heartily at my lack of fortitude. But, at that point, the world could have been laughing. There was no way I was going to Topeka on that tiny little plane.

I did eventually get there. When we arrived, what do you suppose was parked on the landing strip just outside of the terminal at Topeka? Yes, you guessed it, that tiny little four-seater that I had refused to fly in. But, I have a theory that the only reason that they made it is because they did not carry me or the Redención Viva books.

Now, it is going to take a great deal more courage than that and a great deal more fortitude than that to travel the journey of the Christian life. You see, God is asking us to get aboard a vehicle that, in the eyes of the world, is too light for the weight that we need to place upon it. Yet, those who fly on the wings of faith are able to soar to heights that cannot be reached in any other way. Let's face it. Sometimes they have to fly through stormy clouds and through choppy skies. Sometimes they have to fly directly into fierce headwinds of spiritual trial and opposition. To put it simply, it is not easy to live by faith.

But, I have got good news this morning. Lots of people have taken that journey ahead of you. They have reached their destination with distinguished success, by faith. It is very appropriate that the eleventh chapter of the book of Hebrews should sometimes be called the Faith Hall of Fame. For in this chapter are inscribed the names of famous men and women, who practiced the greatest art that is known to man. They practiced the art of trusting God.

You know when you fly the airways of America, you often find yourself in very impressive company. I was on a flight to Atlanta many years ago and a man walked down the aisle toward the first class cabin. I was 99% sure that it was Dr. Martin Luther King. Some years later, I was in Washington, and I recognized the man in the first class cabin as the newly appointed Secretary of Labor in the Carter administration. He spent a great deal of the flight giving an interview to a reporter. Once when I was about to fly out here to Los Angeles, I was sitting in my window seat, and who should sit down next to me but my very distinguished colleague from the Dallas Theological Seminary, Dr. Charles Ryrie and his wife. We marveled that we were not only on the same flight together, but that we had seats next to each other. A flight is always better if you are in good company.

If you let me change the figure of speech for just a minute, the jetliner called Faith is loaded with distinguished passengers. You have many fellow travelers on the journey of Christian living. In the few minutes that remain, I would like to introduce you to just three of your fellow passengers. Because, I think that if you get acquainted with their lives, you will learn a lot about what it really means to live by faith.

The first fellow passenger that I want you to meet is a man you probably will recognize. His name is Abel. Of course, he was a son of Adam and Eve (Gen 4:2). He was also the first man in history to get murdered (Gen 4:8). You say, "Wait a minute, Zane. What possible inspiration could I get from a man who got himself killed? What challenge could there be in the life of someone who was brutally butchered by his own brother?" Quite a bit, I think.

For you see, Abel understood, by faith, one of the greatest secrets which it is possible for a man to understand. Abel understood the way in which it is necessary to approach God. You see, when Cain brought his sacrifice, he brought of the fruits of the ground, he brought some of the things that his own hands had produced (Gen 4:3). God did not want to be approached with that kind of a sacrifice. Abel understood that if God was to be approached, He must be approached with sacrificial blood. He brought animal sacrifices. He brought of the firstlings of his flock (Gen 4:4). By faith, Abel offered a more excellent sacrifice to God than Cain. God bore witness of his gift, and testified that he was righteous. Abel understood the great truth that God is approached through sacrificial blood.

You know there are lots of people in the world today who think they can approach God very much like Cain did. They bring Him their hands, their good works, and their efforts to be good, religious, and worthy. There is not a person on the face of the earth who can be good enough to be accepted by God. If we expect God to accept us, we must come to Him on the basis of the precious blood of Jesus Christ.

In one of the rock galleries on the island of Gibraltar, two soldiers mounted guard one night. One of them was a Christian and the other was a man who was seeking Christ. At midnight, when they were making their rounds, the Christian soldier was meditating on the blood of Christ and on the peace that he had found through faith in that blood. The unsaved soldier was grieving on his fears and doubts.

Suddenly, an officer confronted the Christian soldier and demanded the password. The soldier, without thinking, and speaking just out of the thoughts of his heart, said "the precious blood of Christ." Then, immediately, he corrected himself and gave the official password and the surprised officer passed on. But the words that he had spoken echoed down the rock gallery and bounced off of the solid stonewalls and they fell on the ears of the troubled, seeking soldier, like they had been a message from heaven. It was just as if an angel from the throne had said to him, "the precious blood of Christ".

Do we understand this morning, my friends, that the only real password into the presence of God is the blood of Jesus Christ, which was shed on the cross for our sins? When we come to God to receive eternal life, we come on the basis of that blood, trusting only and completely in what Christ has done for us. Not only when we come to God for salvation, but every time we come to God in prayer, in praise, and in worship, we come not on the basis of our own merit, but on the basis of what Jesus Christ has done for us on the cross.

The life of Abel is an illustration of that profound truth. Even though he was killed by his own brother, he being dead yet speaks. His life is a memorial to the supreme reality that God is approached through the sacrificial blood of Christ. You will not be able to live the Christian life successfully unless you keep that principal in mind. That is your first fellow passenger.

The second fellow passenger is a man you might not know a great deal about. His name was Enoch. This man stands in striking contrast to the man we just talked about, because you see, whereas Abel's life was cut short by the cruel hand of his brother, Enoch's life never ended. He never died. The writer of Hebrews says,

> By faith Enoch was taken away so that he did not see death, "and was not found, because God had taken him," for before he was taken he had this testimony, that he pleased God (Heb 11:5).

Enoch lived in the days that led up to the flood. These were days of growing violence and growing moral and spiritual decay, very much like our own day. Yet despite all of the corruptness and violence around him, Enoch pleased God. He pleased God so well that God simply took him directly to heaven. How did Enoch please God? Well, in the OT, in the book of Genesis, we read a very impressive statement about Enoch. We are told in the book of Genesis, "And Enoch walked with God; and he was not, for God took him" (Gen 5:24).

If Abel is a man who worshipped God by faith, Enoch is a man who walked with God by faith. Enoch had a companion on the pathway of life. They were in company together and they walked along together. When they got to the end of life's road, God said to Enoch, "Don't bother about dying. Just come back home and be with Me." Enoch walked with God.

Anne Sullivan was born in Feeding Hills, Massachusetts in poverty and in affliction. She was also half-blind. When her mother died, she went over the hill to the poor house. But later, at the Perkins Institute for the Blind, a brilliant operation restored her sight. From that time and forward, she devoted herself to the care of the blind. Meanwhile, a little baby was born down south, a little girl who after early childhood would never hear or speak or see. Her name was Helen Keller.

In due time, Helen Keller came under the care of Anne Sullivan. In two weeks, Anne Sullivan taught her thirty words just by spelling them out by touching her hand. Under the tutelage of Anne Sullivan, Helen Keller rose to national prominence and fame. Teacher and pupil became companions. They were inseparable until the day of Anne Sullivan's death. In her darkness, Helen

Keller found a companion who could teach her and who she could trust.

If you really want it, you can have a companion along the pathway of life. Though you cannot see Him, you can trust Him. He can teach you and be with you. By faith, you can walk with God and please God. "But without faith it is impossible to please Him, for he who comes to God must believe that He is, and that He is a rewarder of those who diligently seek Him" (Heb 11:6). Enoch believed deeply in the reality of the living God, and he believed it was worth seeking Him. He believed he could get to know God intimately, because God "is a rewarder of those who diligently seek Him."

Back in my apartment in Dallas, Texas, I have a long-playing record by Mario Lanza on which he sings the charming music of the "Student Prince." Of all of the songs on that record, the one that has touched me the most deeply is the song that is entitled "I'll Walk with God." The words of the song go like this,

> I'll walk with God from this day on. His helping hand, I'll lean upon. This is my prayer, my humble plea, may the Lord be ever with me. There is no death, though eyes grow dim. There is no fear when I am near to Him. I'll lean on Him forever and He'll forsake me never. He will not fail me, as long as my faith is strong, whatever road I may walk alone. I'll walk with God. I'll take His hand. I'll talk with God. He'll understand. I'll pray to Him, each day, to Him. And He'll hear the words that I say. His hands will guide by throne and rod. And I'll never walk alone while I walk with God.

"Enoch walked with God; and he was not, for God took him" (Gen 5:24).

But, there is one last fellow passenger that I want you to meet very quickly before I close. He is undoubtedly the most famous of the three. He is Noah. If Abel worshipped God by faith and if Enoch walked with God by faith, Noah worked for God by faith. Noah worked by faith, because he built the ark. The writer of Hebrews tells us,

> By faith Noah, being divinely warned of things not yet seen, moved with godly fear, prepared an ark for the saving of his household, by which he condemned the world and became heir of the righteousness which is according to faith (Heb 11:7).

Noah lived on the very threshold of the greatest calamity that had ever overtaken the world. He lived at the doorsteps of the flood, and he had no visible evidence that the flood was coming. But, he believed what God said about the coming flood. And because he believed it, he got to work. He built that ark in which his whole family passed safely through the flood (Gen 6:13–8:18). He came out on the other side having become an heir in that select circle of those who lived righteously by faith.

Do I need to tell you that you and I are living on the threshold of the greatest disaster that the world has ever known? The great tribulation is coming according to the prophetic word of God. Seven years of unparalleled calamity in the experience of mankind from which, graciously, we will be saved by the rapture of the Church. If we really believe that deeply enough, then we are going to get to work. We are going to do the things that God has set before us to do.

Charlotte Elliott had a brother who was in the ministry and was trying to raise funds for a school that would minister to the daughters of other clergymen. Charlotte was forty-five years of age and she was in poor health. She could not do anything to help. One day, there was supposed to be a big program, which was designed for fund raising. The night before the program, Charlotte Elliott could not sleep. She tossed and turned, and she really doubted that she would ever be useful to God.

The next morning everybody got up and went to the program. Charlotte Elliott was left at home alone. When she sat alone in her home, she began to meditate on her own weakness. She realized a great truth. She realized that just as her salvation was by faith, so also her Christian life must be lived by faith and trust. She picked up her pen, and she wrote a hymn. The hymn that she wrote has become one of the truly famous hymns of the Christian church. Its title is "Just as I Am". "Just I am, without one plea, but that Thy blood was shed for me. And that Thou bidst me come to Thee, O Lamb of God. I come, I come." Do you realize that that hymn which she wrote is found in literally thousands of evangelistic meetings? Only God knows the number of men and women who have been touched by the words of that hymn, and drawn to personal faith in Jesus Christ.

Noah used his hands to build the ark. Charlotte Elliott used her hands to write a hymn. If you and I are men and women of faith, we are going to use our hands to do whatever God wants us to do. Like Noah, we will become heirs of the future world. We will become partakers and partners with the King in His glorious Kingdom if we work for God by faith.

Uncle Dudley was an elderly gentleman who had lived all of his life in a small West Virginia town. On his seventy-fifth birthday an aviation enthusiast invited him to take an airplane ride over the town, where he had lived his whole life. So they got up in the airplane and they flew around in the airplane and eventually they landed on the ground. When they got down to the runway the pilot turned to Uncle Dudley and said, "Were you scared Uncle Dudley?" "No," came the hesitant reply. Then Uncle Dudley added, "But, I never did put my full weight down."

Do you know that that is exactly what is wrong with some Christians? They never have put their full weight down. Oh yes, they come to Christ through personal faith in Him. But then, when they meet the problems and difficulties and struggles of life, they try to solve them on their own. They do not put their full weight down. They have never really learned that the entire Christian life must be lived by faith and trust. For by faith, we worship God. By faith, we walk with God. And by faith, we work for God.

> Simply trusting everyday. Trusting through a stormy way. Even when my faith is small, trusting Jesus that is all. Singing if my way is clear. Praying if the path be drear. If in danger, for Him call. Trusting Jesus that is all. Trusting as the moments fly. Trusting as the days go by. Trusting Him what'ere befall. Trusting Jesus that is all."[1]

---

[1] Edgar Page Stites, "Trusting Jesus" (1876).

Scripture Index

Genesis
- 2:2-3 50
- 3 50
- 4:2 103
- 4:3 104
- 4:4 104
- 4:8 103
- 5:24 ..... 106, 108
- 6:13–8:18 108

Numbers
- 13:28 47
- 13:32c-33 47
- 14:7b-9 48

Deuteronomy
- 12 50

2 Samuel
- 14:25 57
- 15 57
- 16-17 58
- 18 58

1 Kings
- 12:4-7 24
- 12:8-11 24

Psalm
- 3:5-8a 58
- 8:3-5a 35
- 8:4-6 35
- 8:5b-6 36
- 22 62
- 22:1-2 63
- 22:19-21a 63
- 22:21b 63
- 45:6 21
- 45:7 22
- 95 45
- 95:7b-8a 45
- 110:1 64
- 110:4 64

Proverbs
- 4:23 45
- 11:25b 95

Lamentations
  4:6 86
Matthew
  7:24-27 11
  26:41 62
  26:42, 44 62
  26:39 62
Mark
  10:45 95
Luke
  22:44 62
John
  3:16 20
  5:24 59
  6:35 78
  6:37b-39 79
Acts
  16:31 59
  20:35c 94
Romans
  4:5 .... 50, 61
Philippians
  2:8b-11 15
  2:9-11 64
Ephesians
  2:8-9 50
2 Timothy
  2:12 .... 28, 41
Titus
  3:5a 61
Hebrews
  1:1-2a 9
  1:2-3a 13
  1:3b 14, 15

1:3c 20
1:7 21
1:8 .... 21, 22
1:9 .... 22, 23, 25
1:9b 23
1:13 .... 15, 17, 28, 51, 60
1:13-14 60
2:5 34
2:8 36
2:10 38
2:18 39
3:1 25
3:7-11 45
3:7b-8a 49
3:12 .... 45, 48
3:14 25
4:9-10 52
4:11 53
4:14-16 66
4:16 14
5:7 63
5:7-8 61
5:9 61
5:12 72
5:13 73
5:14 74
6:4-6 76
6:7-8 79
7:1 90
7:21b 90
7:24-25a 66
10:4 90
10:14 90
10:19-22a 88
10:19-25 .... 87, 88
10:22 91
10:23 .... 9, 12, 92, 93
10:23a 76, 91

10:24	95
10:24-25a	94
10:25b	94
10:29	86
10:30	80, 81
10:30-31	87
10:35	82
10:36-37	96
10:36-37a	93
11:1	100
11:5	105
11:6	107
11:6a	100
11:7	108
11:23	81
12:1c	40
12:2	40
12:28	25, 29

Revelation
2:26-27	27
3:21	27, 52

Subject Index

Apostasy......................... 76, 88
Authority 51
Believe..............11, 13, 20, 33,
    48-49, 53, 59, 65, 70, 79,
    107, 109
Blood... 20, 34, 39, 55, 62, 86,
    88-90, 104-105, 109
Branches 44
Bread 48, 78-79
Children......21, 36, 44, 46-48,
    50, 75, 84, 98
Commitment..7, 9, 26, 28, 76
Confess.............. 15, 25-26, 64
Confession...9, 11, 65, 76, 81,
    91-93
Confidence ... 9, 25-26, 28, 82
Cross.....15, 38, 40, 42, 62-63,
    78, 89-90, 105
Cup 62
Death......... 11, 15, 23, 32, 37,
    39, 44, 48, 59, 61-64, 77,
    86-87, 105, 107

Discipline......................79-80
Disobedience..................... 53
Disobey.............................. 69
Doubt........................... 45, 99
Drink.................................. 76
Everlasting life.............. 20, 59
Faith 1-2, 8, 12, 15, 20,
    26, 28, 33-34, 39-40, 50,
    57, 61, 66, 71-72, 76-79,
    81, 88-90, 95-97, 100,
    102-110
Faithful........ 12, 28, 81, 92-93
Fall away 76
Finished 51-52, 91
Fire 13-14, 21-22, 32,
    34, 65, 79-81
Flesh 34, 39, 55, 61, 63,
    88-89
Follow.............. 60, 67-68, 101
Fruit 50
Gospel 85
Grace ... 14, 29, 34, 39, 50, 66,

79-80, 86-87, 91
Growth 80-82
Holy Spirit 76, 78, 82
Inheritance . 15, 46, 49, 51-53
Inspiration 41, 103
Judas 62
Judge 80-81, 87
Judgment 59, 61, 86
Lamb 109
Law 24, 31, 86
Life 2, 5, 8-9, 11-12, 14-15,
    17-18, 20, 27-28, 32, 34,
    42, 44-45, 52-54, 56, 59,
    63-64, 66, 70-71, 75-76,
    78-80, 83-84, 93, 95, 97,
    99-100, 102-103, 105-
    107, 109-110
Light 19, 28, 102
Lord 12, 15, 17, 22, 24, 28,
    42, 46, 48, 51-53, 58-60,
    63-64, 67-68, 71, 80-81,
    85, 87, 89-94, 107
Lost 13, 37, 44, 53, 70, 79,
    88, 95, 97
Love 28, 32, 71, 94-95, 98
Mature 71, 74
Ministry 77, 90, 109
Miracle 81-82
Obedience 62-63, 65, 76
Prayer 62-63, 66, 89, 105, 107

Repentance 77-78
Rest 43, 48-54, 101
Righteous 79-80, 104
Righteousness . 22-23, 50, 61,
    72-73, 108
Sacrifice 15, 90, 103-104
Save 55, 58-59, 61, 63,
    65-66
Saved 34, 39, 50, 53-55, 57,
    59, 61, 65-66, 70-71, 79,
    86, 100, 108
Savior 15, 59, 66, 71, 85, 90
Seek 107
Seeking 104-105, 107
Sin 37, 46, 66, 80, 86, 90
Submission 87, 93
Submit 14
Suffering 31, 33, 39, 41,
    62, 65
Surrender 38, 87
Transformed 70-71
Truth 16, 20, 78, 87,
    104-105, 109
Unfaithful 99
Witness 54, 85, 104
Works ... 27-28, 35-36, 50, 52,
    61, 94-95, 104
Worship 21-22, 87, 89, 94,
    105, 110

Printed in Great Britain
by Amazon